When I finally decided to buy a pool table for my home, the "decision" was really a no-brainer, and thus my criteria were strikingly simple: it was a quite-rare, six-legged Brunswick Alexandria, it had been built circa 1910, and the price was just this side of miraculous. As to its functionality, I had already been playing on it for years.

Rarely, however, is buying (or selling, for that matter) a pool table that kind of slam-dunk. There are important considerations well beyond the grasp of most dilettante shoppers. And now there's a superb book, pragmatically titled *Buying or Selling a Pool Table*, by Mose Duane, that can turn naive shoppers into expert ones.

Mr. Duane has also authored *The Billiard Guidebook* and *Dirty Pool: Playing to Win*, with a fourth volume, *Pool Table Maintenance and Repair*, due soon. Unlike most self-published efforts, this book is well organized as well as meticulously written and edited. In this volume, he analyzes rails, playing surface, frames and cabinets, finish, cushions, pockets, cloth and accessories, with valuable insights that could potentially save hundreds if not thousands of dollars. There are some very wise inserts titled Buyer Tips, Seller Tips, and Words of Experience. He also includes some well-intentioned pool jokes that are so old, Cro-Magnon Man was beating them out on hollow logs ("I quit playing pool once. It was the most terrifying weekend of my life."). But it's easy to forgive that particular quirk.

For example, the book offers you an 18-page chapter of wisdom on rails alone. Did you know there are three kinds? Would you know which would be best for your application, and why? Or whether to specify rails mad of hardwoods, finished woods or laminated plastic? And should they be attached to the table frame or the slate itself, and why? Mr. Duane knows all those answers, along with every other conceivable particular on rails, and he passes that knowledge along in clear, direct terms. His many line-drawing illustrations are equally clear and easy to follow.

His chapter on cabinets and frames is equally useful (and so is every other chapter in the book). For example, I would have had no clue that there are two basic types of cabinets. Again, Mr. Duane gives you all your options, clearly illustrated and described, along with valuable recommendations.

As a final reason for owing this fine work, I'll simply quote one of several "Words of Wisdom" asides that are also part of it: "Last week, I delivered a table that someone had paid a thousand dollars too much for. When I delivered it, I said, 'You know, there's a book available that explains the differences between tables that would've saved you hundreds of dollars.' His answer: 'I didn't want to spend the twenty-five bucks.'"

If you're considering a purchase or sale, or know someone who is, this book is about the biggest favor you could do for either of you. It's quite remarkable that no one has approached this subject in this kind of depth before, but Mr. Duane has made up for lost time.

Buying or Selling A Pool Table is available for $24.95 form Phoenix Billiards . . .

—George Fels, Billiard Digest

Buying or Selling a Pool Table, by Mose Duane. If you're going to buy a pool table (new or used—or sell one—you need this book, it's that simple. Why skimp on the price of the book when investing two, or three, or four thousand dollars (or more)? It wouldn't be a bad idea for someone who already owns a table to have a copy, as well. In fact, we can recommend that.

The book is very well organized, which makes it easy to use, and there's additional information about buying the accessories that go with your table (chalk, rack, balls, lights, dust cover, etc.)

Very few table buyers look underneath the table, and those that do usually don't have any idea what they're looking for. It's like the used car buyer who lifts the hood and says, "Yep, engine's there." That's only natural, because buying a pool table isn't an everyday experience, and there's no reason anyone should have picked up that knowledge in general conversation. Duane's book has that info, however. After reading it you'll know what's good, and what's not so good, about any pool table you're looking at. That could make all the difference in the world. From playing surface to leg attachment, you'll know what you're buying before you plunk down your hard earned cash.

Bottom line: If you're going to buy or sell a new or used pool table you'd better have this book.

—Thomas C. Shaw, Pool & Billiard Magazine

Buying or Selling a Pool Table is a handy, concise, and informative book, chocked full of helpful hints and pertinent illustrations on buying or selling a pool table.
　　—Jack Baker, Indoor Outdoor Sports,
　　Memphis, Indiana

Buying or Selling a Pool Table should be required reading for anyone in the business, or anyone wanting to learn about buying or selling a pool table.

Buying or Selling a Pool Table was written in an easy to read, straightforward language.

Buying or Selling a Pool Table has chapters that are organized in ten logical divisions intended to help readers quickly understand the components that make a buy, no buy decision, and to help sellers get top dollar for their tables.

Buying or Selling a Pool Table expertly explains what to look for when buying or selling any pool table.
　　—Keith Colby, Arizona Billiards.

Buying or Selling a Pool Table is more than a book on buying and selling. It also covers tables and equipment in such a way that anyone can thoroughly understand them.

Buying or Selling a Pool Table is the book for you if you want to buy the right table at the right price, or sell a table and get full price.

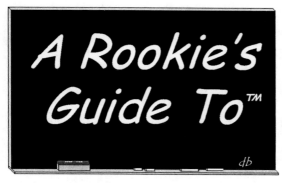

BUYING OR SELLING
A POOL TABLE

TEN ESSENTIAL COMPONENTS TO
CONSIDER WHETHER NEW OR USED

Mose Duane

Phoenix Billiards

6133 W. Port-au-Prince Lane
Glendale, AZ 85306
phoenix**billiards**.com

The purpose of this manual is to educate and entertain. It is designed to provide information in regard to the subject matter covered. It is sold with the understanding that the publisher and author are not engaged in rendering legal or professional services. If legal or other expert assistance is required, the services of a competent professional should be sought. Although the author and publisher have used care and diligence in the preparation, and made every effort to ensure the accuracy and completeness of information contained in this manual, we assume no responsibility for errors, inaccuracies, omissions, or any inconsistency herein. Any slights to people, places, or organizations are unintentional. The author and publisher shall have neither liability nor responsibility to any person or entity with respect to any loss or damage caused, or alleged to be caused, directly or indirectly by the information contained in this manual. If you do not agree with the terms in this paragraph, please return this manual, with proof of purchase, within thirty days of its purchase for a full refund of the price of the book.

Illustrated by the author
Cover photographs courtesy of
                    Connelly Billiard Mfg, Inc.
Cover by Erika A. Diehl, www.erika.org
Printed by Print Partner, Tempe, Arizona, USA

Publisher's Cataloging-in-Publication
(Provided by Quality Books, Inc.)

Duane, Mose.
   A rookie's guide to buying or selling a pool table :
ten essential components to consider whether new or
used / Mose Duane.
-- 1st ed.
   p. cm.
   Includes index.
   LCCN: 2001118806
   ISBN: 0-9678089-4-4

   1. Pool (Game)--Equipment and supplies. 2. Billiards
--Equipment and supplies. I. Title.

GV899.D83 2002   794.7'0297
                          QBI01-201215

ACKNOWLEDGMENTS

I would like to thank all those who encouraged and harassed me into completing this book.

Especially:

Craig Connelly, Connelly Billiard Manufacturing, Inc., for his encouragement, and of course for the pictures of his excellent pool tables used for the cover.

Steve Lunsford, Steve Lunsford Billiard Slates, for his belief in my endeavors, from the beginning.

Nancy and John Katrakis, Print Partner, whose advice and guidance were invaluable.

Keith Colby, who is forced to read my stuff before anyone else.

Tim Acree, who was brutal in his evaluation of my writing.

Tom Shaw, Pool & Billiard Magazine, for his kind words.

George Fels, Billiard Digest, also for his kind words.

Karen, my wife, who should have taken a hammer to my computer years ago, but did not.

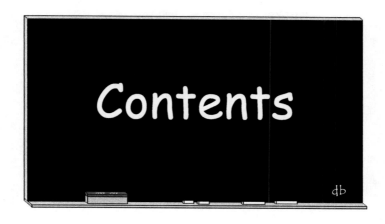

Contents

i

Introduction

Buying or selling a pool table can be haphazard for anyone who doesn't know what to look for, or how to look for it. I don't intend to amuse you with advice on how to negotiate, or how to buy for less or sell for more than market value. There are far too many of those books available already. My intentions are to simply show you what to look for to insure that you pay or receive a fair price for any pool table. In order of importance, then, I have listed what I think are the ten essential components that you should consider, and why, to make it easier for you to put a value on a pool table.

Buyers who are overwhelmed with their first impression often overlook some of these components. Compared to most furniture, pool tables are massive and can be overbearing in their appearance. Buyers might experience love at first sight because a junk table looks impressive or ornate, or they might walk away from a treasure because the cloth is ratty. Sellers might let a treasure go dirt-cheap because they refuse to spend a few dollars to have it cleaned up, or they simply don't know what they have.

So, if you're a buyer, don't let first impressions influence a buy, no buy decision. Pool tables need to be approached from the standpoint of their essential components, looking at each separately and critically, and weighing each as to which is important and which can be ignored. If you're a seller, these components need to be assessed to determine which can be feasibly repaired, and which can be prudently ignored.

Of course, all components become important, or even critical, if the table is inexpensive or manufactured cheaply, where any one component could represent most of the table's price. In this case, a buyer can reject the table if any component is not up to par, and a seller needn't worry about repairs. On the other hand, the same components of a well-made table are often the least expensive parts of the table. In this case, the table can be purchased (at a discount) even though some flaws exist, as long as the rest of the table is in acceptable condition. Indeed some deficiencies— worn out pockets, cloth, cushions, etc.—can be easily and cheaply replaced or repaired and should not devalue a table a great deal, if it was a solidly built table to begin with. From a seller's standpoint, these inexpensive deficiencies should be corrected before selling to increase the appearance and perceived value of the table.

Further, pool tables constructed with quality can withstand a fair amount of abuse, and are usually bargains when purchased used. They can be bought for about half what a new table would cost. Once they have been cleaned up, re-cushioned, and covered with new cloth, they often look as good as they did when new, and will certainly play just as well. And they will be worth top dollar.

Conversely, cheaply made tables are not normally bargains when purchased used, or new as far as I'm concerned, when you would be far better off buying a good used table. In the past, I have argued that cheaper tables had their place in the world because they made pool tables available to those who couldn't otherwise afford them. I want to rescind that. It now seems silly to me that anyone would buy a cheap or low-quality pool table when the same money could buy an inexpensive new or good-quality used table. To differentiate, almost all manufacturers of quality pool tables also make an inexpensive model or two. These tables maintain some of the quality of their counter-parts—wood rails, slate playing surface, gum rubber cushions, etc. Cheap, low-quality tables, on the other hand, are those made of particle board or pressed fiber board, often including the playing surface. I've seen new non-slate tables delivered that were so badly warped that it was impossible to level them. They don't even make good toys for kids. Frankly, they simply aren't worth the material it takes to make them, let alone giving someone a profit. Although some cheap tables may look and play reasonably well when new, they literally fall apart with time and use. Thin laminates crack and peel. Softwoods shrink and splinter. Particle or fiberboard warp, swell, and loosen around screws and bolts. Frames and rails become wobbly and can require a good deal of time and money to repair. They have no real resale value. Department stores, sporting goods stores, and other stores that don't specialize in pool tables typically sell these tables. As a matter of fact, it would be rare to find a low quality table in a store that specializes in pool tables and billiard equipment.

As a buyer, whether buying a new or used table, you should never shop strictly brand names. As stated earlier, most manufactures, even the best known, make a line of inexpensive home or home-style tables, as well as their line of quality home and commercial tables. Also, shop several dealers, even when buying from an individual. Let the dealers explain the best features of their various brands and models. As a seller, however, you should tout your particular brand, since that's the one you're selling. Talk it up. Know why it's better than the others.

When buying a table from reputable dealers, they will not misrepresent the table in any way— size, condition, worth, etc. However, when buying from an individual, be careful. Some will, if not lie, certainly stretch the truth to insure a sell. Others may not intentionally misrepresent the table, but will honestly not know the difference between a sound table and one that is virtually falling apart. They may not even know whether the table is slate or some other material, or even if it's a pool table or a snooker table.

In any case, if you aren't informed, whether buying or selling, you could get stung. On the other hand, if you are an informed buyer, you may be able to find the "steal." But you won't find it from an informed seller!

For years, the billiard industry has been trying to drop the use of the word "pool" in reference to the game. The reason of course is the unsavory stigma the word conjures up. After all, the word starts with P, that rhymes with T, and that stands for trouble, as the song goes. In that sentiment, then, "billiard or billiards" was used throughout my first book; *The Billiard Guidebook*: A Complete, on the level, Manual of Maintenance, Specifications, and Playing; to encompass all billiard games and tables.

That proved to be cumbersome, however. So throughout this book, I have chosen to use the term pool and pool table to cover all the various games and tables that are often called pocket billiards.

Furthermore, with a great deal of modifications in text and format, I have extrapolated this book from *The Billiard Guidebook*. And, like its predecessor, it is well illustrated with some of the same clear figures, and seeded with some reference tables, along with "WORDS OF EXPERIENCE," "BUYER TIP," and SELLER TIP" sidebars.

Also, if you are not acquainted with frequently used pool or billiard terms, a short glossary has been placed at the end of the book. Take a few minutes to scan any unfamiliar terms. It will make your reading much easier.

And, finally, if you feel anything important has been left out of this book, or was not thoroughly and clearly expounded upon, please feel free to write.

Enjoy
Mose Duane

Other books by Mose Duane

A Rookie's Guide To
Playing Winning Pool
From Beginning to Advanced Players

A Rookie's Guide To
Pool Table Maintenance and Repair:
A Manual for Assembling, Re-covering,
Re-cushioning, Leveling, and Repairing

A Rookie's Guide To
Pool Table Assembly
Detailed and Illustrated Instructions
for Most Pool Tables

All books are available at bookstores,
on-line book sellers, pool table supply stores,
or directly from **PHOENIX BILLIARDS**
1-800-449-0804   1-602-843-0804
www.phoenix**billiards**.com
www.rookies-guide.com

Words of Experience

I was introduced to the world of pool at the local Boy's Club in Columbus, Indiana at an impressionable age of ten or so. They had one 9-foot table that was always in desperate need of repairs because no one seemed willing or capable of doing the work. Imagine a ten-year-old even considering the lack of maintenance on anything, let alone a game he was just introduced to. But there I was, learning to play on a table with more ruts and valleys than a golf course. In spite of that, I learned enough about playing during those early years to later hustle the game when I was in the army at Fort Campbell, Kentucky, and then in College at Indiana University.

I have stayed with pool, first in Indiana, where my then partner and lifelong friend "Indy" Turner and I opened a twenty-five-table poolroom we called *The Velvet Rail*, then twenty-two years in Phoenix. I have made or refurbished hundreds of tables and moved, recovered, and re-cushioned thousands of others in those years. I can look at a table and tell its general history including how many nuts, bolts, and screws it takes to hold it together.

Pool is a game of which I have made a profession. It has been good to me. Now I have twenty plus years of pool table knowledge, a pocket full of change, and feel obligated to give something back. This book, then, is one of my contributions. It can cut days off the process of buying or selling a table at a fair price.

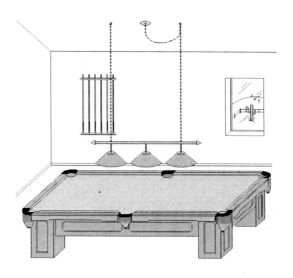

Chapter 1. Pool Room

Few homes are built with a poolroom in mind, so finding a room of ideal size is rare. However, there are two ways to get around the size constrictions without poking holes in the drywall. One is a smaller table. The other is a shorter cue.

11

Although room size isn't actually part of a pool table, it is the most important component of buying or selling a table.

If you are selling a table, your chances go up immensely if you can show the potential buyer why and how it will work within the constraints of a particular room. Don't try to push a certain size table because it's "regulation," or "it's what everybody is buying." A table should fit the room and lifestyle of the buyer, not some vague notion of what is "regulation," "standard," or "popular." If you're buying a table, knowing what will fit and where it will fit, will expand your possibilities.

Seller Tip

Your chances for a sale go up immensely if you can show the potential buyer why and how your table will work within the constraints of a particular room.

Although most major tournaments are played on $4^{1}/_{2}$ x 9 foot tables, any size table can be regulation depending on the regulating body, and any size or style can be a bargain and can be enjoyed, as long as it conforms to the room.

There are three related room size or table size dimensions that should be considered: distance from walls, room dimension, and foot clearance.

Buyer Tip
If you're buying a table, knowing what will fit and where it will fit, will expand your possibilities.

DISTANCE FROM WALLS

Optimally, a room should be large enough to leave 5 feet of unobstructed clearance along each edge of the table. No wall, post, pillar, bar, table, or counter should obstruct a player or cue (Figure 1-1).

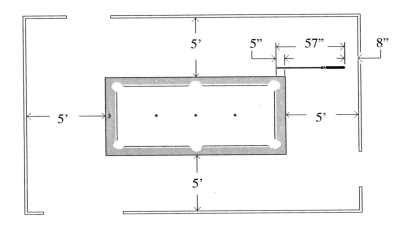

Figure 1-1 *Ideal table distance from walls*

A standard cue is 57 inches long, 3 inches shy of 5 feet, and most rails are approximately 5 inches wide. This allows 8 inches for stroking between the butt of the cue and the wall when the cue ball is at its worse position—frozen to a cushion—and the shot is perpendicular to the rail and wall. With 5 feet around the table, using a standard cue, there are no shots that cannot be made due to wall interference.

Normally, however, most shots are at an angle to the rail with the cue ball away from the cushion. Because of that, the cue clearance can be cut by 6 inches and allow minimal, but satisfactory, playing conditions. Those 6 inches are per side and end, which is a decrease of a foot in overall room size. So $4^{1}/_{2}$ feet clearance per side and end is, if not ideal, quite playable using a standard cue.

ROOM DIMENSION

Table 1-1 shows the optimum and minimum room dimensions for most pool table sizes.

A good rule-of-thumb for figuring the optimum room size is simply adding 10 feet to the table size. For example, a 4 x 8 table needs a 14 x 18 room, a 5 x 10 table needs a 15 x 20 room, and so forth. Subtract a foot overall to obtain the minimum room size.

Or, if starting with the room, take its dimensions and subtract 10 feet. A 13 x 16 room, for example, will optimally accommodate a 3 x 6 pool table, and a $3^1/_2$ x 7 minimally.

STANDARD 57 INCH CUES

Table Size	Optimum Room Size	Minimum Room Size
3 x 6	13' x 16'	12' x 15'
$3^1/_2$ x 7	13' 6" x 17'	12' 6" x 16'
44 x 88	13' 8" x 17' 8"	12' 8" x 16' 8"
4 x 8	14' x 18'	13' x 17'
$4^1/_2$ x 9	14' 6" x 19'	13' 6" x 18'
5 x 10	15' x 20'	14' x 19'
6 x 12	16' x 22'	5' x 21'

Table 1-1 *Room dimensions*

Room dimensions can also be cut substantially by using a shorter cue, and figuring the distance from the wall as the same as the cue length. For example, using a 54-inch cue, instead of a 57-inch as in Table 1-1, a playable room size can successfully be decreased to 54 inches around the table, a 48-inch cue will decrease the room size to 48 inches around the table, and so forth. (By the way, using this criterion, the optimum distance for a standard 57-inch cue can be cut to 57 inches, instead of the recommended 5 feet, saving 3 inches.)

Buyer Tip

Because there are no regulations that require a 57-inch cue, a cue can be cut to any length. Shorter than 48 inches, however, the cue becomes too small for good control.

Because there are no regulations that require a 57-inch cue, a cue can be cut to any length. Shorter than 48 inches, however, the cue becomes too small for good control.

To figure the room size using a shorter cue, double the cue length and add the overall table size. A 3 x 6 table using 48-inch (4 feet) cues, for example, can be set up in a room that is 11 x 14 (3' + 4' + 4' = 11') and (6' + 4' + 4' = 14'). Don't let this string of numbers fog your mind. Two 48-inch cues equals 8 feet, and the table is 3 feet wide, that's 11 feet, etc. Easy stuff.

Table 1-2 shows the room dimensions for 54-, 52-, and 48-inch cues.

NONSTANDARD CUES

Table size	54" Cue Room size	52" Cue Room size	48" Cue Room size
3 x 6	12' x 15'	11' 8" x 14' 8"	11' x 14'
$3^1/_2$ x 7	12' 6" x 16'	12' 2" x 15' 8"	11' 6" x 15'
44 x 88	12' 8" x 16' 4"	12' 4" x 16'	11' 8" x 15'4"
4 x 8	13' x 17'	12' 8" x 16' 8"	12' x 16'
$4^1/_2$ x 9	13' 6" x 18'	13' 2" x 17' 8"	12' 6" x 17'
5 x 10	14' x 19'	13' 8" x 18' 9"	13' x 18'
6 x 12	15' x 21'	14' 8" x 20' 8"	14' x 20'

Table 1-2 *Room dimensions using cue lengths*

FOOT CLEARANCE

The floor beneath and around the pool table also needs to be clear of obstacles such as ledges, steps, benches, chairs, boxes, camping gear, toys, etc. This clearance should be a minimum of 4 feet from the outer edge of the table (Figure 1-2).

If this clearance isn't provided, a proper cuing stance cannot be obtained. Tripping over, kicking, and stepping around floor obstructions and furniture detracts greatly from the playability of the table and concentration on the game.

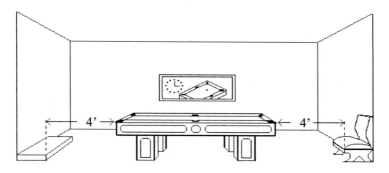

Figure 1-2 *Distance from obstacles*

Also, using the area beneath the table for storage, however convenient, can be an obstruction, not to mention tacky.

FLOORS AND CEILINGS

There is no recommended flooring material or ceiling height for a poolroom. A pool table can be leveled on any kind of floor—tile, wood, carpet— it doesn't matter. Some installers use carpet as an excuse for sloppy work, but the truth is any table can be leveled on any carpet, and carpet has the advantage of being quieter than other flooring. Coarse and uneven tiles like saltillo are as easy to level on as is concrete and smooth tiles. Upstairs rooms, however, tend to settle from the weight of a pool table, so the table should be re-leveled every month or so until settling stops.

Buyer Tip

Any table can be leveled on any carpet, and carpet has the advantage of being quieter than other flooring.

Although there is no recommended ceiling height, it really should be over eight feet. Anything lower can actually get in the way of the cues, and will get perforated by the cue tips.

CONCLUSION

Ideally, the room size should be $4^1/_2$ to 5 feet larger than the pool table, and over 8 feet high. Also, allowing at least 4 feet of foot clearance around the entire table is desirable.

If short cues are used, a 48-inch cue is the lower limit.

Rank poolrooms in the following order:

Ideal: At least 5 feet clearance around the table.

Good: $4^1/_2$ feet clearance around the table.

Okay: 1. Five feet clearance around
                     most of the table with some
                     areas where a short cue is
                     needed.
                     2. Using short cues with cue
                     length spacing around the table.

Poor: Anything under 4 feet around
                     the table.

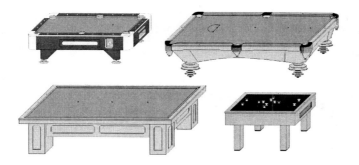

Chapter 2. Tables

In a general sense, there are four kinds of "billiard" tables—pool, snooker, carom, and rebound—each reflecting the game played on the table. Each is covered here, in basic terms, to eliminate most of the confusion between them. A table is the sum of its parts, of course, but like the room size, it must be considered as an important component of buying and selling.

POOL TABLES

Pool (pocket billiard) tables are the most common tables, if not in the world, then certainly in the United States.

The most noticeable distinguishing features of pool tables are pocket size and width of opening, and flat pocket facings (Figure 2-1).

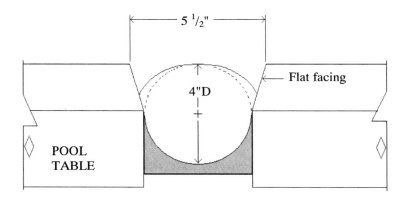

Figure 2-1 *Distinguishing features, center pocket*

Basically, there are four kinds of pool tables—coin-operated, commercial, home, and rebound (Bumper)—although I've separated the home tables into two categories, quality and low quality, because of the vastness of material and craftsmanship used in their construction.

Coin-operated Pool Tables

Coin-operated pool tables are generally found in bars, taverns, poolrooms, and other places that want to charge on a per game basis.

These tables have a box style cabinet with detachable rails and $^3/_4$-inch one-piece slates. Within a few inches one way or the other, coin-op tables are 3 x 6 or $3^1/_2$ x 7 feet in size (Figure 2-2).

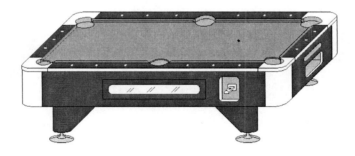

Figure 2-2 *Coin-operated table*

Commercial Pool Tables

Commercial pool tables are heavily constructed to provide solid playing characteristics for commercial poolrooms, multi-table recreation rooms, and major tournaments.

Commercial pool tables usually have hidden, all-wood frames with all-wood rails laminated with hard burn and mar resistant plastic like Formica or Micarda (Figure 2-3). The sizes of commercial pool tables are 4 x 8 feet and $4^1/_2$ x 9 feet, with $4^1/_2$ x 9 being the prominent size. The playing surfaces of commercial tables are 1 inch, three-piece slate that has a $^3/_4$-inch wood backing. Commercial tables may have exposed leather pockets, interior pockets, or a ball return system.

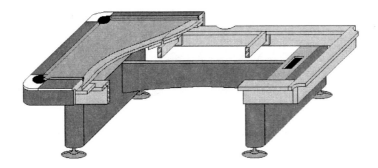

Figure 2-3 *Commercial pool table*

Home Pool Tables (quality)

Home pool tables aren't built as heavy as commercial tables, but can still be of excellent quality, and some are being used commercially. The majority of quality home tables have exposed cabinets with a good tough finish that should hold up in the home for years (Figure 2-4).

Home tables are usually 3 x 6 feet, $3^{1}/_{2}$ x 7 feet, oversize 4 x 8 feet, and some are $4^{1}/_{2}$ x 9 feet, although a standard 8-foot version, 44 inches x 88 inches, is fast becoming the prominent size. These tables have $^{3}/_{4}$ inch to 1-inch slate, with 1 inch being the preferred thickness.

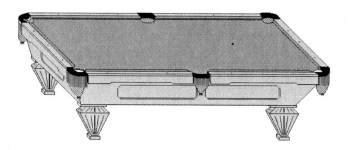

Figure 2-4 *Quality home pool table*

Most Asian imported tables, although they look more like high quality tables at first sight and may have 1-inch slates, would fall into a category somewhere between good and low quality because the inferior materials used in their construction.

Home Pool Tables (low quality)

At the other end of the home table range are the low quality tables (Figure 2-5). These tables are made of softwoods, particle or fiberboard, or both, and most are laminated with paper-thin wood grain plastics. Low quality home tables have $^3/_4$ inch slate (usually undersize) or particle board playing surfaces, and are usually 44 x 88 inches or smaller. Most of these are department store tables and lack in durability and playability. Be diligent in your assessment. If a table looks low quality, it is.

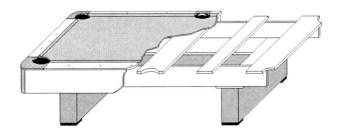

Figure 2-5 *Low quality home pool table*

Outside Pool Tables

Earlier models of outside pool tables were made of wood covered with a thick vinyl like Naugahyde. Even the playing surface was covered with the thick vinyl. These tables played poorly and didn't hold up long, especially outside. Water crept into the cracks and crevasses and had no way out. The wood, screws, and staples deteriorated rapidly (Figure 2-6).

Newer versions of outside tables are made of aluminum, fiberglass, and other resins, with the playing surface covered with a thinner material like Sunbrella. These newer tables fair much better from a durability and playability standpoint than the older models, although not close to a regular pool table covered with good billiard cloth.

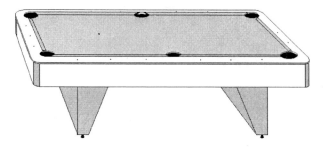

Figure 2-6 *Outside pool table*

Outside pool tables are usually 44 x 88 inches in size. Some variant of a resin composite playing surface is used on several models, but most are simply non-outside materials like particle or fiberboard, or plywood.

Playing Field

The playing fields of all pool tables, no matter their size, are laid out the same so will help distinguish them from other, especially snooker (Figure 2-7). The long string is an imaginary line that divides the width of the playing field in half. It aligns with the center sights of the head and foot rails.

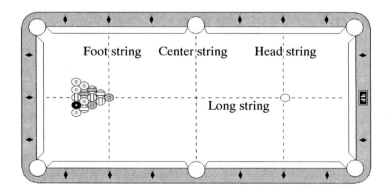

Figure 2-7 *Pool table layout*

The center string line divides the length of the playing field in half. It should align with the center of each center pocket.

Head and foot strings quarter the length of the playing field, and aligns with the center sights of their respective side rails. The head, center, and foot spots are located where the head, center, and foot strings intersect with the long string.

The area between the head rail and the head string is the area of balk (also known as the kitchen); this is where the cue ball is placed when a foul occurs, or during the initial break. The foot spot is the point at which the apex of the triangle of balls is racked. Generally, only the foot spot is marked, and string lines are not.

Playing field dimensions are measured from cushion nose to cushion nose, and are listed in Table 2-1.

Table size	Playing field
3' x 6'	36" x 72"
$3^{1}/_{2}$' x 7'	40" x 80"
44" x 88"	44" x 88"
4' x 8'	46" x 92"
$4^{1}/_{2}$' x 9'	50" x 100"

Table 2-1 *Pool table playing field dimensions*

SNOOKER TABLES

There are also commercial and home snooker tables, although most are built to a higher standard than low quality pool tables.

For snooker tables, the distinguishing features are their large size, small pockets and pocket openings, and cushions that curve into the pocket with no facings (Figure 2-8).

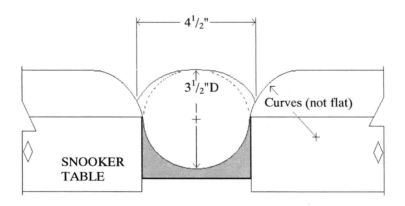

Figure 2-8 *Notable features, center pocket*

Snooker tables can have either all-wood hidden frames or exposed cabinets. The sizes of snooker tables are $4^1/_2$ x 9 or 5 x 10 feet, with 5 x 10 being the most prominent. The playing surfaces of quality snooker tables are 1 inch, three-piece slate that is backed by wood. Snooker tables may have exposed leather pockets, interior pockets, or a ball gully system.

Except for the rounded pocket facings and smaller pockets mentioned above, and the playing field layout, snooker tables can and do look exactly like commercial or high quality pool tables (Figure 2-9).

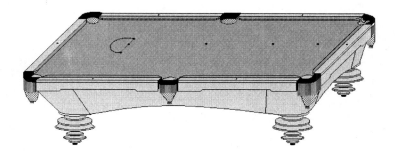

Figure 2-9 *Snooker table*

Playing Field

For snooker table layout, the long, foot, and center strings are found in the same manner as those on a pool table. The head string, however, has a specific dimension from the head rail, which does not necessarily quarter that end of the table. Head, center, and foot spots are located at the intersection of the string lines. All spots are marked, but string lines are not (Figure 2-10).

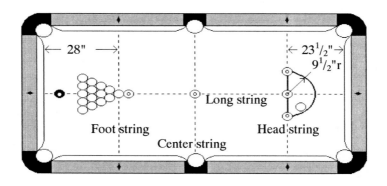

Figure 2-10 *Snooker Layout, 5' x 10' table*

Within the D-ring is the area of balk; this is where the cue ball is placed when a foul occurs, or during the initial break. The D-ring should always be marked on the table.

The foot spot is the point at which the apex of the triangle of red balls is racked.

A snooker table also has a 7-ball spot at the foot of the table, a 4-ball spot at the head spot, and a 2-ball and 3-ball spot where the head string intersects the arc of the D-ring. The relative positions of these spots, and size of the D-ring, change somewhat depending on the size of the table.

Playing field dimensions are measured from cushion nose to cushion nose, and are listed in Table 2-2.

Table size	Playing field
$4^1/_2$' x 9'	50" x 100"
5' x 10'	56" x 112"

Table 2-2 *Snooker playing field dimensions*

CAROM TABLES

There are also commercial and home carom (billiard) tables, although, like snooker tables, most are built to a higher standard than low quality pool tables.

The distinguishing features of carom tables are their large size, and their lack of pockets. Carom tables can have either all-wood hidden frames or exposed cabinets (Figure 2-11).

These sizes are 5 x 10 feet and 6 x 12 feet, with 5 x 10 being the prominent size in the United States. The playing surfaces of quality carom tables are 1 inch, three-piece slate with a wooden backing. Carom tables do not have pockets.

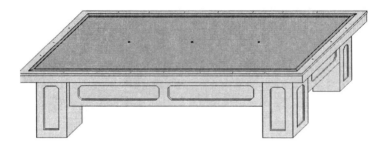

Figure 2-11 *Carom table*

Playing Field

Carom tables are generally laid out in the following manner. The head, foot, and center strings are imaginary lines that are found in the same manner as those on a pocket billiard table.

Head, center, and foot spots are located at the intersection of the string lines (Figure 2-12).

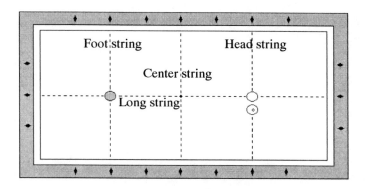

Figure 2-12 *Carom layout*

All spots are marked, but string lines are usually not. Like pool and snooker, the playing field dimensions are measured from cushion nose to cushion nose, and are listed in Table 2-3.

Table size	Playing field
5' x 10'	56" x 112"
6' x 12'	70" x 140"

Table 2-3 *Playing field dimensions*

REBOUND TABLES (BUMPER POOL)

Rebound pool began as Bumper Pool, which is a registered trademark of the Valley Company of Bay City Michigan. The Bumper Pool version is played on an approximate 3 x $4^1/_2$-foot rectangular table with twelve bumpers and two pocket holes (Figure 2-13).

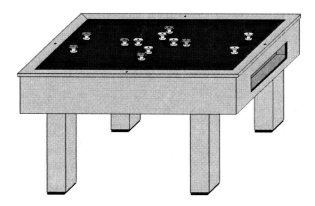

Figure 2-13 *Bumper Pool table*

Rebound pool tables are usually hexagon shaped with six rails instead of four and some have only 10 bumpers. This shape is used to facilitate a removable card or game surface that sets on top.

Quality rebound and Bumper Pool tables have slate playing surfaces, gum rubber cushions, and an all-wood cabinet or frame, but most are low quality tables that are made of particle or fiberboards, including the playing surfaces.

Playing Field

Balls are aligned two on each side of the opposite color pocket hole and the marked ball in front of the pocket hole (Figure 2-14). Playing field dimensions are measured from cushion nose to cushion nose, and, depending on cushion width, are usually around 28 x 44 inches, with a slate dimension of 32 x 48 inches.

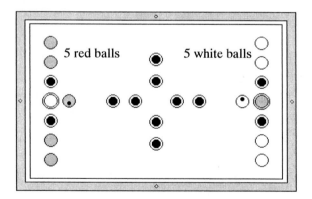

Figure 2-14 *Bumper Pool layout*

CONCLUSION

First and foremost, you should know the difference between the various tables. If you're selling and don't have any idea what kind of table you have, don't just assume it's a "pool table" and sell if for the first available dollar. If it's a commercial table or a snooker table, it may have more value than a home pool table. If you're buying, know what you're paying for. From a monetary standpoint, you should

Seller Tip

If you don't have any idea what kind of table you have, don't just assume it's a "pool table" and sell if for the first available dollar.

also be aware of the style and construction of the table you are buying or selling. I've delivered many tables that should have gone directly to the dump, and a few I would have gladly paid twice what the buyer paid.

Further, as a buyer, you should buy and use the type table you intend doing most of your playing on. There are some who believe that if you practice on a snooker table, because of the large size, small balls, and pockets, it will improve your pool game. It will certainly improve your snooker game, but there's no indication that it will help you with pool. Similarity, playing on a 9-foot pool table will not specifically help on 8-foot or 7-foot tables. Certainly any playing on any table will help improve your overall performance, but playing on one table

Buyer Tip

If you're going to play in tournaments, buy and play on tournament tables. If you intend to play in bars, buy and practice on a bar table. If you're going to play snooker . . . and so on.

won't necessarily help on another. So, if you're going to play in tournaments, buy and play on tournament tables. If you intend to play in bars, buy and practice on a bar table. If you're going to play snooker, buy a snooker table . . . and so on.

Rank all tables in the following order:

Ideal: 1 inch (or thicker) three-piece oversize slate with a $^3/_4$ inch backing board. All wood frame, rails, and legs. High quality, slick finish.

Good: 1 inch (or thicker) three-piece oversize or standard size slate with a $^3/_4$ inch backing board. All wood frame, rails, and legs. High quality finish or mar and burn resistant top rail.

Okay: 1. $^3/_4$ inch (or thicker) one-piece oversize slate with a $^3/_4$ inch backing board. All wood frame, rails, and legs. Good quality finish or mar and burn resistant top rail.

2. $^3/_4$ inch one-piece or other undersized, non-backed slate. All wood rails with rail bolts, not lag screws. Particle or fiberboard, or plywood apron, frame, or legs. Good quality finish or mar and burn resistant top rail.

Poor: All particle or fiberboard construction with thin, rough finishes or laminates.

Words of Experience

A few years ago, a lady called me to move a pool table she'd bought from a guy who inherited it when he purchased his house. She wanted to surprise her husband with a pool table he always wanted. I picked the table up in the evening and delivered it the next morning while he worked, and had been instructed not to call for fear of alerting him to his surprise. The next morning, when I delivered the table, she was shocked when I informed her that she'd purchased a snooker table instead of a pool table.

Apparently, no one knew the difference.

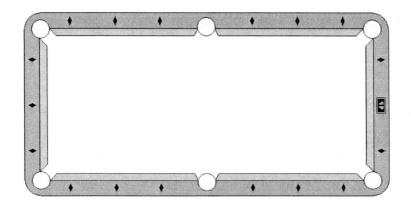

Chapter 3. Rails

There are three kinds of pool table rails
commonly used today—flat rails, T-rails, and
detachable rails (Figure 3-1). Detachable rails are
generally found on coin-operated tables, T-rails on
antique tables, and flat rails on most modern
tables.

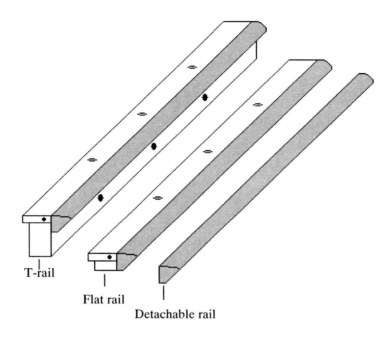

T-rail

Flat rail

Detachable rail

Figure 3-1 *Rails*

Top quality rails are made from select hardwoods that give the table a lively and solid playing characteristic. Some are finished woods, while others are laminated with plastic.

Although some quality rails have durable laminates over hardwoods, which makes a good-looking, functional rail, other lower quality rails are constructed from softwoods, particle board, or fiber board, and use inexpensive, paper-thin plastics that look good for awhile, but are subject to peeling and skinning.

Three problems develop with the use of softwood, particle board, or fiber board rails. First and foremost is the apparent inability of these materials to hold glue. Laminates and cushions may peel or sag, leaving either ugly rails with blisters and bubbles, or rails that will not rebound properly. Second, these materials are not capable of holding screws or nails over time. Rails become loose, aprons fall off, pockets become detached, and so on. Third, instead of the feather strip (see Figure 3-4) compressing to hold the rail cloth in place, the feather strip grove spreads open. This often permanently damages the rail, or, at the least, it allows the rail cloth to pull away from the top rail.

DETACHABLE RAILS

Detachable rails are generally found on coin-operated tables (Figure 3-2), although a few "home-style" tables also have them. A detachable rail is simply a wooden (tacking) strip with cushion rubber and facings glued to it; it is that portion of the assembly covered with billiard cloth. The top rail is permanently (more or less) attached to the frame, thereby becoming part of the cabinet.

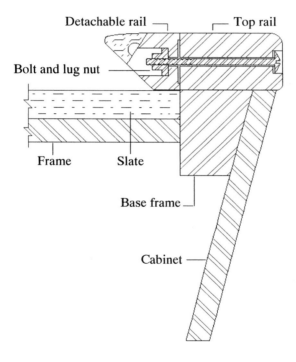

Figure 3-2 *Detachable rail*

Generally, the detachable part of the rail is attached to the top rail in three different ways: side mount, bottom mount, and metal clip (Figure 3-3).

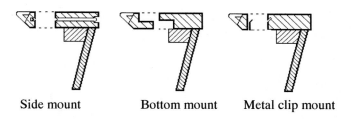

Side mount   Bottom mount   Metal clip mount

Figure 3-3 *Detachable mounts*

The most common is the side mount rail that has three or four long screws that penetrate the width of the top rail and screw into the detachable portion of the rail. The bottom mount rail has an L-shaped tacking strip that slides beneath the top rail and is secured from the bottom. The metal clip mount rail has an unusual metal fastener that slides into the middle of the top rail allowing the bottom to hinge beneath the base where it is fastened. The bottom and metal clip mounts are becoming rare but some still exist, and are usually found on home-style tables.

The advantage of the detachable rail method over the T-rail or flat rail is the ease in which an owner can disassemble the table to move or recover it. The disadvantage is that detachable rail tables are built with undersized slate that extends only to the edge of the rail; the rail is attached to the frame instead of the slate (see Figure 4-3). The problem with this system is a rail assembly that allows poor ball action.

T-RAILS

T-rails are most often found on older tables. They are constructed by bonding three pieces of hardwood—the top rail, the tacking strip, and the base—together in, more or less, a T-shape (Figure 3-4).

The top rail is made from a decorative wood, such as rosewood, ash, oak, mahogany, and so forth. Occasionally the top rail is made of a lower

grade wood and laminated with a high quality
(usually wood grain) plastic, like Formica.

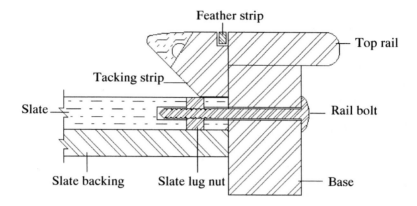

Figure 3-4 *T-rail*

The tacking strip and base are most likely made
of poplar.

T-rails are attached with bolts from the side,
screwing into lug nuts that have been leaded into
the slate. This system of attachment is one of the
oldest, but certainly not easiest, cheapest, or best.

The rail bolts can be hex-head with standard
threads, but most antique tables have a
nonstandard, thrust-head bolt with two holes that

accepts a fork type tool instead of a standard wrench or socket.

The bolt heads are covered with either individual ornamental rosettes or a decorative apron that covers the entire rail base (Figure 3-5).

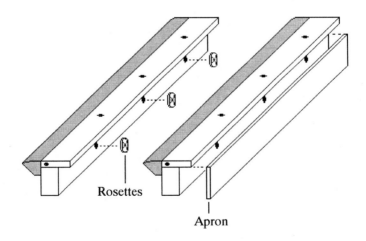

Rosettes

Apron

Figure 3-5 *Apron or rosettes*

FLAT RAILS

Flat rails are usually constructed by bonding two pieces of wood together—top rail and base—

but can be cut from one block of wood. The top rails of high quality tables are made from $2^1/_2$ to $5^1/_2$ x $^3/_4$-inch hardwoods like rosewood, ash, oak, maple, etc., and the base from a hardwood such as poplar. Less quality rails could have a top rail laminated with a good quality plastic, but underneath it can be made from almost anything: softwoods, particle board, pressed fiber board, or some combination, with the base also made from a similar material (Figure 3-6).

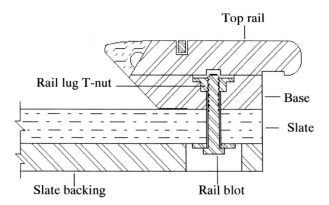

Figure 3-6 *Flat rails*

Quality flat rails are attached to the table with rail bolts that penetrate up through the slate and into the rail, which has been equipped with lug nuts. These are T-nuts, plate nuts, or screw nuts.

T-nuts (Figure 3-6) and floating plate nuts (rail 4 in Figure 3-7) are implanted between the top rail and the base to create a more solid attachment.

Screw nuts are simply treaded nuts that are screwed into the rails (rail 3 in Figure 3-7). Plate nuts are affixed to the rails by wood screws (rail 4 in Figure 3-7).

Some manufacturers bypass the use of lug nuts altogether by using woodscrews or lag screws (rail 1 in Figure 3-7). In time, these can become loose, causing a weak connection.

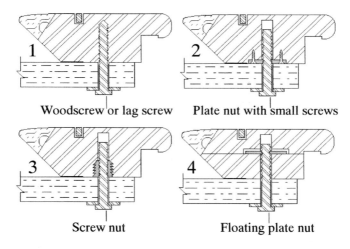

Figure 3-7 *Flat rails with various attachments*

Even given that, properly attached flat rails are the better of the three kinds—flat, T, and detachable—because of the positive bottom attachment to the slates.

The ends of some flat rails are cut square to accept leather pockets or rail castings, while others are mitered to fit together much like a picture frame (Figure 3-8).

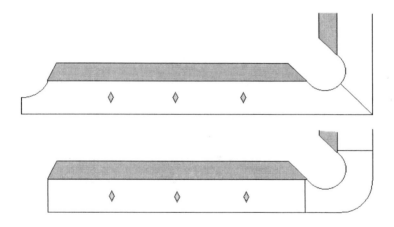

Figure 3-8 *Mitered and squared corners*

Mitered joints allow pockets or pocket liners to be attached inside the rail assembly. The converging mitered joints are usually covered with plastic caps or metal castings.

The uni-constructed rail is a flat rail with mitered joints in which all six rails are constructed as one unit and cannot be separated.

All flat rails have an apron to hide the edge of the slate (Figure 3-9).

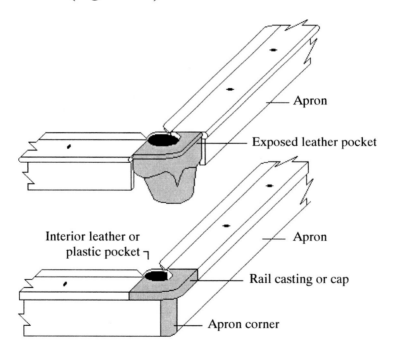

Figure 3-9 *Flat rails with aprons*

Aprons are either glued permanently to the base, are screwed onto the base or frame, or are attached with metal brackets or wood blocks. Except for rails with leather pockets, aprons are joined at the corner with plastic or metal apron corners, and rails are joined with rail caps or castings.

SIGHTS

Sights can be inlaid into the top rail with a variety of materials. Some older tables have ivory sights, but the most common material is mother-of-pearl, or plastic that resembles mother-of-pearl. Inexpensive tables may have ink-screened sights, or upholsterers' tacks, or cover plates that hide rail bolts that penetrate the top rail in precisely the sight area. Ideally, though, sights should be seen and not felt, they should be as smooth as the top rail.

Whatever the material, sights were originally strategically located on the rails for aiming purposes (Figure 3-10).

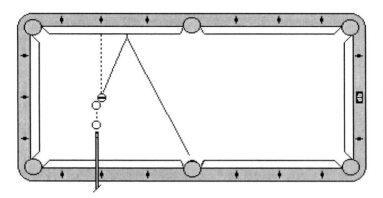

Figure 3-10 *Sights*

There is a mathematical scheme called *The Diamond System* that can be used to figure angles for bank shots using the sights.

The process was originally intended for carom play but works well for any kind of pool table or game. The system employs "english" and immediate mental calculations during a shot and is, therefore, generally ignored. For more on english see *A Rookie's Guide to Playing Winning Pool* or visit phoenix**billiards**.com.

For more information, The Diamond System is explained in several "how to make shots" books and the Billiard Congress of America's (BCA) official rules book. BCA's booklet can be purchased from most pool table supply stores or directly from: Billiard Congress of America, 4345 Beverly Street, Colorado Springs, CO 80918.

RAIL BOLTS

Rail bolts or screws (often called hanger bolts) are the hardware that holds the rail assembly to the table bed. There are four types of rail bolts.

1. Detachable rail bolts pass through the side of the top rail into lug nuts affixed in the detachable rail (Figure 3-2).

2. T-rail bolts pass through the side of the rail's base and fasten into lug nuts implanted in the slate (Figure 3-4).

3. Flat rail bolts go up through the bottom of the table bed (usually penetrating the slate) to fasten into lug nuts in the rails (Figure 3-6).

4. Lag bolts or woodscrews simply screw into the rail without the use of lug nuts (Figure 3-7).

CONCLUSION

There are thousands of beautiful tables sold every year that don't play worth a nickel because the rails are inferior. Look at the rails carefully to determine how they were constructed and from what materials. Are they hardwood, softwood, laminated wood, or particle or fiber board? Are they attached to the slate or frame? Are they secured by bolts and lug nuts, or lag screws? For playability, rails should be made from hardwoods and bolted directly and solidly to the table slate.

Buyer Tip

For playability, rails should be made from hardwoods and bolted directly and solidly to the table slate.

After visually checking the rails, swiftly roll a ball against a cushion. The table should sound solid. If it sounds "hollow" the rails are probably attached to the frame instead of the slate, or they are simply loose. If you're selling the table, make

sure all screws and
bolts are tightened.
It'll pay dividends.

All rails should
have aprons that match
them in quality, both
in material and
appearance.

Seller Tip

*Make sure all screws and
bolts are tightened.
I'll pay dividends.*

Rank rails in the following order:

Ideal: Solid hardwood flat rails that are
                bolted to the slate.

                Four bolts per rail on 8-foot or
                larger tables are a plus.

                Sights should be smooth, and
                diamond shaped sights are an esthetic
                plus.

Good: 1. All wood flat rails laminated with
          top-quality plastic like Formica,
          bolted to the slate.

          2. Solid hardwood T-rails that are
          bolted to the slate.

          3. All wood T-rails laminated with
          top-quality plastic like Formica,
          bolted to the slate.

Okay: Particle or fiber board flat rails
          laminated with top-quality plastic like
          Formica, bolted to the slate.

Poor: 1. All wood, or particle or fiber board
          flat rails or T-rails attached to the
          slate with lag screws or wood screws.

          2. All wood flat or T-rails attached to
          the frame.

          3. Particle or fiber board flat or T-rails
          attached to the frame.

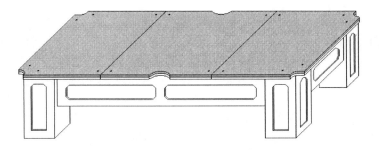

Chapter 4. Playing Surface

Essentially, there are four kinds of pool table playing surfaces: slate, marble, honeycomb, and particle or fiber board.

Playing surfaces should be $29^1/_4$ to 31 inches off the floor.

PARTICLE OR FIBER BOARD

A particle or fiber board playing surface is simply a sheet of one or the other, usually 3/4 inch thick (but could be up to 2 inches), set in the table to take the place of slate. It is a cheap and ineffective means to manufacture a table. Particle and fiber board tables wobble, warp, chip, ding, and sound cheap. They are extremely vulnerable to water, so be aware of water marks, stains, wet basements or garages, and so on.

A few years ago there was a table bed called "Slateen," and now one called "Slatron." Although these department store tables sound like they could be some high-tech man-made slate, they are simply particle or fiber board, some even painted slate-gray, and should be avoided.

HONEYCOMB

Honeycomb beds are made with 5 or 6 inch wide strips of corrugated cardboard (like cardboard boxes) laid on edge, in a honeycomb fashion. The cardboard is then sandwiched between two thin sheets (usually $^1/_4$ to $^3/_8$ inch) of particle board to make a 5 or 6 inch thick bed. These beds usually stay relatively level as long as they do not get wet. However, they are light, and susceptible to being bumped and moved as a player shoots.

Honeycomb tables are particle board tables so they will also wobble, warp, chip, ding, and sound cheap. They are also vulnerable to water, so be aware of water marks, stains, wet basements or garages, and so forth.

MARBLE

Marble, like slate, is a metamorphic rock that has been successfully used for pool table playing surfaces for years. Marble is flat, true, and has substantial weight. It is, however, more brittle than slate, and, consequently, more susceptible to cracking or breaking.

SLATE

Slate is a gray, fine-grained, metamorphic rock that splits into natural slabs when mined. It is rigid, flat, not susceptible to warping, and ideal for pool table playing surfaces. The majority of today's slate is quarried in Italy where it is split, cut to

size, and diamond honed flat. Often pocket cutouts
and bolt holes are bored before it is crated and
shipped. Because it is inexpensive and naturally
abundant, slate is by far the best and most popular
pool table playing surface.

Usually pool table slates are cut in one or three
pieces (Figure 4-1). Some older tables have two or
four pieces but that's rare. If a table is constructed
and assembled properly it makes little difference,
from a levelness standpoint, whether or not the
slate is one or more pieces. However, one-piece
slates are generally undersize and, therefore, do
not extend beneath the rails, so are not considered
regulation by popular sanctioning boards.

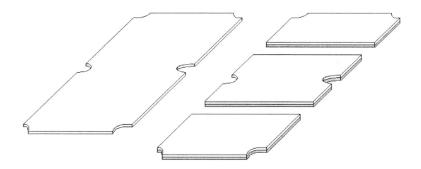

Figure 4-1 *One-piece and three-piece slate sets*

Some 7- and 8-foot tables have a one-piece slate playing-surface and others have three pieces. However, because of weight, all 9-foot and larger tables have multiple slates.

Often each individual slab of a three-piece slate set is backed with a $^3/_4$-inch thick tacking board. The tacking board is attached to the bottom perimeter of each slate to help prevent warping, and to allow a way to tack the bed cloth to the table. With unbacked slate the cloth must be attached to the frame or glued to the slate itself. Although some sanctioning boards require a tacking board for regulation tables, neither system is better than the other.

Slates on most pool tables are $^3/_4$ to 1, or $1^1/_8$ inch thick. On occasion, an older table might have a $1^1/_4$ or $1^1/_2$ inch slate, but rarely would anything thicker be found. Once the cloth has been stapled to the tacking board, though, the slate appears to be $^3/_4$ inch thicker than it actually is. That is probably the reason for stories of 2 and 3-inch thick slate tables. (One exception I can think of is Connelly's 2-inch Altima). The two real advantages to thicker slate are a heavier, more stable table, which is less likely, and sometimes impossible, to be bumped around; and the slate is less likely to warp or crack.

In some cases, the edges that join the three pieces of slate are doweled to keep the pieces flush to each other, then honed at the same time to make a matched set. This provides an extremely accurate means of leveling. Because of expense, however, some slates are center screwed to the frame instead of being doweled, and, without wedging and work, are only as level as the frame (Figure 4-2).

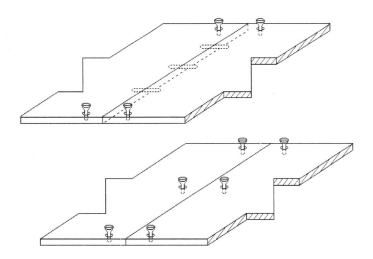

Figure 4-2 *Doweled or screwed slate sets*

Slates are sized according to the way tables are designed. T-rails attach to the side of the slate. Because this was one of the original designs, the slate is considered "standard size." In order for flat rails to attach to the slate without changing the dimension of the playing field, the slate is extended beneath the rails. This larger slate is designated "oversize." Other slates end just below the cushions, and the rails attach to the frame

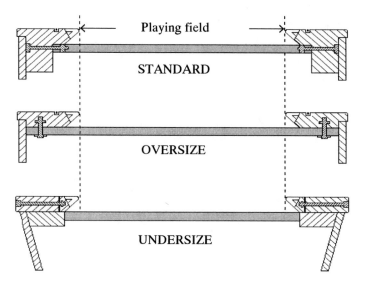

Figure 4-3 *Slate sizing*

instead of the slate. This smaller slate is referred to as "undersize." Figure 4-3 illustrates the same playing field sizes using standard, oversize, and undersize slates.

CONCLUSION

Although slate can be replaced and sometimes repaired, it often costs more than the price of the table, but not always. This is one of those cases where you must know or learn the value of the table, whether you are buying or selling.

Seller Tip

Although slate can be replaced and sometimes repaired, it often costs more than the price of the table, but not always.

Stay clear of a non-slate table; it will have little value, and if the rest of the table is in poor condition, it will have no value.

Often, if the cloth is still on the table it's hard to tell a slate bed from a non-slate. Rap on it, if it sounds like rock it probably is, after all slate is rock. Likewise, if it sounds like particle or fiber board, it is. If rapping does not help, crawl under the table and look at the bottom of the bed. Does it look like slate, or particle or fiber board? Careful, though, don't be deceived. Some particle and fiber board are painted slate-gray and look like slate. If all

Buyer Tip
Stay clear of a non-slate table; it will have little value, and if the rest of the table is in pool condition, it will have no value.

else fails, take a small knife, nail, or some similar object and scratch the bottom of the playing surface; that will instantly identify what it is made of.

Once slate has been determined, look at the structural cross members that support the middle of the slate. One member across the center of the table usually indicates a one-piece slate, and two members dividing the table into thirds usually indicate a three-piece slate. Also, looking beneath the table, a slate division can be seen between the center and corner pockets, between the apron and the outside of the cabinet or frame.

Strictly speaking, one is not better than the other as long as the rails are attached to the slate, but this is extremely rare on a one-piece slate table. So, whether one-piece or three-piece, make sure the slate extends beyond the edge of the frame and the rails are bolted to the slate. This does not always hold true and should be visibly verified. Older three-piece slate tables have standard size slates with rails that attach to the side, but still to the slate. Attaching the rails to the slate is a critical difference for players looking for a solid, positive rebound.

Slates can, and do, warp. There are two ways to check for slate warpage. One is to set a ball at one end of the table and a couple of inches from the side rail. Then, using no english, cue the ball straight toward the other end of the table. Cue it only fast enough to make it travel the length of the table without rebounding. Watch the ball to see which way it rolls off. Do the same for the other side, going toward the same end, and note the roll-off of that side. If both sides roll true, the slate is true.

If both sides roll left or right, at approximately the same amount, the table is not level but the slate is probably true (Figure 4-4).

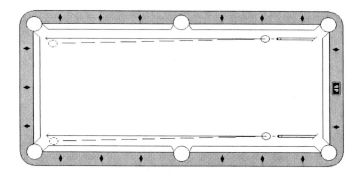

Figure 4-4 *Slate roll-off*

However, if both balls roll toward the center, the slate is sagging; or, if both balls roll away from the center, the slate is bowed. Check both ends.

The second way to check for slate warpage is to remove the bed cloth and lay a 4-foot carpenter's level across the slate surface, end-to-end, side-to-side, and cater-cornered. Tilt the level on one long

Seller Tip

Screwing down the high areas of the slate, and simultaneously wedging the low areas can often correct warpage.

edge and look beneath it. The degree of warpage, if any, can be seen by the amount of space between the level and slate. Small waves around .005 of an inch, about the thickness of two sheets of typing paper, are acceptable.

Screwing down the high areas of the slate, and simultaneously wedging the low areas can often correct warpage. But unless the table has some other great value, like being a priceless antique, it is usually advisable to pass on one with a warped slate.

Slates can also crack and separate either by mishandling or natural fissures. Most slate cracks are hairlines and not always plainly

Buyer Tip

A little water sponged across the slate surface will make cracks appear like they have been painted on.

visible. A little water sponged across the slate surface, however, will make cracks appear like they have been painted on. Often, cracks can be repaired with two part epoxy and clamps. Also, slates with cracks that do not affect the slate's levelness are usable, as long as the slate is solidly screwed to the frame.

Rank slate in the following order:

Ideal: 1. 1-inch (or thicker) three-piece oversize slate with $^3/_4$ inch backing board.

                2. $^7/_8$ or $^3/_4$ inch three-piece oversize slate with $^3/_4$ inch backing board.

Good: 1. 1-inch (or thicker) three-piece standard size slate with $^3/_4$ inch backing board.

                2. $^3/_4$ inch three-piece oversize slate with backing board.

3. $^3/_4$ inch (or thicker) three-piece oversize slate without backing board.

Okay: 1. $^3/_4$ inch (or thicker) one-piece oversize slate.

2. $^3/_4$ inch one-piece undersize slate (rails attached to the frame).

Poor: 1. Honeycomb playing surface of any thickness.

2. Particle or fiber board playing surface, no matter how thick or what name is given to it.

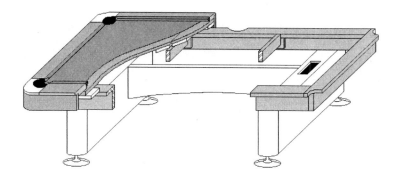

Chapter 5.
Cabinets and Frames
Legs and Pedestals

Pool table frames are as varied as are table manufacturers, but fall into two general categories. One is a table in which the cabinet is also the frame; the exposed portion of the table supplies the support for the slate and table. The second category has a hidden frame; the exposed portions are decorative and supply no, or very little, support.

Within the first category of the cabinet supporting the table, there are three styles: classic, tapered, and box. The hidden frame category also has three styles: boxed-beam, beam and slat, and board. The names given here to the various styles of frames simply reflect their appearance, or the manner in which they were constructed.

Cabinets and frames must be solidly built to withstand not only the weight of the playing surface, but also any side load applied from normal play without wobbling or displacement.

Pool table cabinets and frames are supported by one of two means: legs or pedestals. Other than aesthetics, there is no apparent advantage or disadvantage to one or the other when they are well constructed. Both have been around for years, and have always looked and worked fine.

Just like the cabinets and frames, legs and pedestals must be solidly built to withstand not only the weight of the playing surface and frame, but also any side load applied from normal play without wobbling or displacement.

CABINETS

Cabinet tables are those in which the exposed portion of the table supplies the support for the playing surface and table.

Classic Cabinet
The classic cabinet can be found virtually anywhere in the world, and has not changed much, if any, in hundreds of years. The frame is built on four or six legs with supporting members bolted between them making a rectangular shaped frame (Figure 5-1).

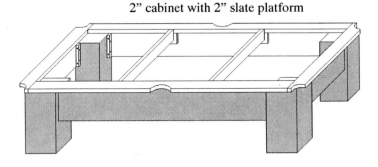
2" cabinet with 2" slate platform

Figure 5-1 *Classic four-legged cabinet*

Even though this classic style has been around as long as pool tables have been in use, it has one basic design flaw. Because the legs were designed at the extreme ends of the frame, over time the weight of the slate forces the center to sag, in some cases as much as half an inch or more. Some manufacturers remedied the problem by introducing six-legged tables, but they are more expensive and as much trouble to level as is a sagging frame.

Figure 5-7 shows a typical six-legged table.

Although the legs depicted here are the classic square legs, this frame in not limited to that style. The legs could be cylindrical, Queen-Ann, claws, lion's paws, tapered, and so on.

Tapered Cabinet

Another exposed table is the tapered cabinet, so named because of its shape. This style is usually a uni-cabinet constructed table that tapers in toward the bottom (Figure 5-2).

These frames also come with a variety of leg shapes: rectangular, cylindrical, Queen-Ann, claws, lion's paws, tapered, etc. Also, the cabinet can be cut with scrollwork, cambers, and routed designs, but it is still a basic taper style cabinet.

1 to $1\frac{1}{2}$ " cabinet with $\frac{3}{4}$ to 2" slate platform

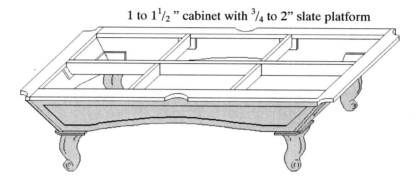

Figure 5-2 *Tapered cabinet*

Considering strength versus lightness, the tapered cabinet is probably one of the best-designed cabinets, if lightness is indeed a plus. It does, however, have a propensity to warp cater-cornered causing the table to wobble corner to corner, often making leveling difficult. Because of its versatility and simplicity, this frame is the most common being built today.

Also, many tapered tables have undersize slate, which means the rails are attached to the frame, as opposed to oversize slates where the rails attach solidly to the slate.

Box Cabinet

The box cabinet is also a uni-cabinet constructed table and it too can taper toward the bottom, but not always. It differs from the tapered cabinet in that the top rails are contained within the cabinet, or is part of the cabinet.

Box cabinets are durable, made to take excessive abuse, and are easier to transport and install than most. Consequently, most coin-operated tables are this style (Figure 5-3).

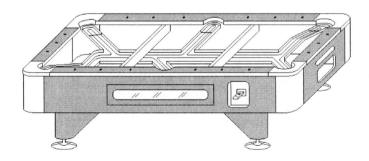

Figure 5-3 *Box cabinet*

HIDDEN FRAMES

The other category of tables is the hidden frame; the exposed portions of the cabinet are cover-ups, usually called blinds or aprons, which produce no support for the tables.

Boxed-beam

The massive L-shaped beams of a boxed-beam frame make it the heaviest style frame built (Figure 5-4). The most famous of this type frame is the Brunswick Gold Crown, introduced in 1959.

2" frame members with 2" slate platform

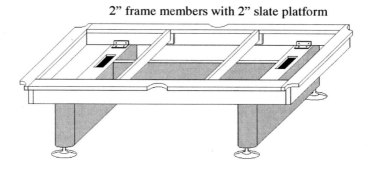

Figure 5-4 *Boxed-beam frame*

Long side beams extend the length of the frame and are bolted together with end beams. The center of the frame is a grid-work of cross beams.

Beam and Slat Frame

The beam and slat frame consists of two or three beams that run the length of the frame with three or five slats bridging them (Figure 5-5). Unbacked slate is laid directly onto the slats, which double as slate tacking boards. These frames are usually made from inferior materials, and are found on less expensive home tables.

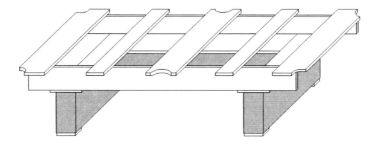

Figure 5-5 *Beam and slat frame*

Board Frame

The board frame is also found on home tables. It is simply 1 x 8 inch (or such) boards, usually plywood, particle board, or fiber board, set on edge and bolted together to form a rectangular structure (Figure 5-6). Cross boards are added to make a very rigid frame that can support its playing surface quite effectively. An unbacked playing surface is screwed to the frame and the bed cloth is glued to the edges of the playing surface, no tacking board is used.

$3/4$ " frame board with no slate platform

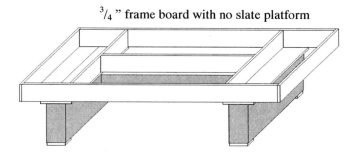

Figure 5-6 *Board frame*

LEGS

If a table has four or six individual supports, it is said to have legs. Legs can be square (Figure 5-7), rectangular, cylindrical, Queen-Ann, tapered, or whatever, as long as they are individually attached to the table.

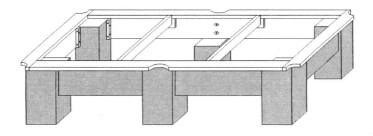

Figure 5-7 *Six-legged cabinet*

Legs should be attached directly and solidly to the frame or cabinet. Thin and flimsy metal corner brackets tend to flex allowing the table to shake and wobble, often more than slightly (Figure 5-8).

If the legs are attached with metal brackets, make sure the brackets are solid with rolled stiffening edges. However, even those have a tendency to wobble. Be skeptical.

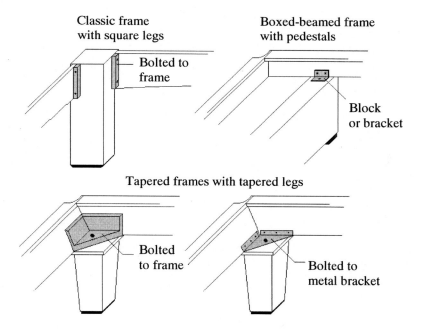

Figure 5-8 *Leg and pedestal attachments*

PEDESTALS

Pedestal supports are usually two rectangular boxes, one at each end of the table, extending the width of the frame. Properly set toward the center of the table to accept the weight distribution evenly, pedestal supports rarely let the frame sag. Also, having a stretcher beam spanning between the two supports helps reduce frame sagging and end-to-end wobble (Figure 5-9).

Contemporary tables can have some version of a single center support that would be considered a pedestal, but they usually aren't very stable.

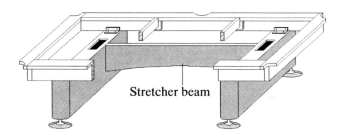

Figure 5-9 *Pedestal with stretcher beam*

CONCLUSION

Generally, a cabinet's function is twofold. One is to support the slate without bowing, sagging, or swaying. The other is to add to the overall appearance of the table. Some cabinets are as well made and beautiful as any fine piece of furniture. They are expensive to repair or refinish, so must be taken care of properly.

Buyer Tip

Look for a cabinet that has an overall look of quality. If the table looks cheap, it probably is, and if it looks expensive, it probably is.

Look for a cabinet that has an overall look of quality. If the table looks cheap, it probably is, and if it looks expensive, it probably is. However, it is not always easy to tell the difference, especially if the table is sitting in a dark room, by itself.

Usually a solid wood cabinet is a better value than one laminated, but not always. High-end commercial tables are usually high-grade hardwood laminated with high-quality plastic, like

Formica. However, a buyer must be aware of low quality tables made from softwoods, particle board, or fiber board that are laminated with paper-thin plastic.

Seller Tip

Make sure the legs are fastened solidly to the table so it does not shake and wobble.

Cabinet tables tend to be more stylish than frame tables, which have a boxy look. A frame's function is the same as the cabinet, which is to support the playing surface without bowing, sagging, or swaying.

The best frames are those that are solidly constructed from a good hardwood like poplar, but frames made from other materials are acceptable, if well constructed.

Frames can only be seen from beneath the table, so crawl under and look. Does it appear flimsy or solid? Is it made of wood, or particle or fiber board?

There are some particle and fiber board tables that function fine, but they shouldn't demand a premium price, and tables with cheaply made, under-built frames should be avoided.

For support, legs or pedestals are as important as the frame. For appearance, they are as important as the cabinet. Whether the table has legs or pedestals is important only in styling. What you should look for then, besides style, is sturdiness.

Sellers should make sure the legs are fastened solidly to the table so it does not shake and wobble, and buyers should stay clear if they are flimsy.

Pedestals should have a stretcher board between them to prevent end-to-end wobble.

The pedestal table is often considered second-rate. That attitude comes from the fact that most inexpensive tables are supported by pedestals. However, there are some fine tables manufactured with pedestals. The Brunswick Gold Crown is an excellent example. Beneath its massive frame are two pedestals that are properly set for correct weight distribution, and are connected by a substantial stretcher beam. The frame never bows or sags (see Figure 5-9).

Rank cabinets and frames this order:

Cabinets:

Ideal:	Solid hardwoods like oak, ash, maple, cherry, mahogany, etc.
Good:	1. All wood with wood laminate.
	2. All wood with top-quality plastic laminate like Formica.
Okay:	Particle or fiber board laminated with top-quality wood laminate. But it must be a uni-cabinet with wood rails and wood legs or pedestals.
Poor:	Particle or fiber board covered with paper-thin vinyl.

Frames:

Ideal:	All wood, preferably poplar. Steel frames, as long as the other major components are wood.

Good: Laminated wood beams;
                poplar, plywood, etc.

Okay: Sheet metal or board
                beams, if the rest of the table is
                all wood.

Poor: Particle or fiber board slats and
                planks, which usually means
                the rest of the table is also
                particle or fiber board.

Legs and Pedestals

Legs and pedestals should be attached solidly and directly to the frame or frame member, and ranked in the following order:

Ideal: 1. Solid hardwoods like oak,
                ash, maple, cherry, mahogany,
                etc. Legs can be carved, Queen
                Anne, lion's paw, claw and ball,
                etc.

                2. All wood, straight, tapered,
                etc.

Good: 1. All wood laminated with top-quality wood laminate.

             2. All wood laminated with top-quality plastic like Formica.

Okay: 1. Particle board laminated with top-quality wood laminate.

             2. Particle board laminated with top-quality plastic like Formica.

             3. With reservations, legs attached by heavy metal corner brackets with rolled stiffening edges.

Poor: 1. Particle or fiber board laminated with paper-thin plastic.

             2. Thin sheet metal corner or leg brackets with no reinforcement edges.

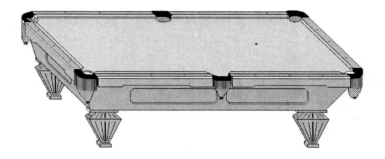

Chapter 6. Finish

There are a variety of pool table finishes, some are superior, most are quite acceptable, and others look good when new but don't hold up over the long haul. The superior finish is one like an expensive hard lacquered "piano" finish. An example of a finish that looks good but doesn't hold up is one with a coat or two of non-sanded polyurethane or a synthetic, painted on wood grain finish. And, an acceptable finish is one that has been properly sanded, stained, two or more coats of lacquer or polyurethane applied and sanded between each coat to give the finish a smooth look and feel.

CONCLUSION

Look for dings, scratches, and mars in the rails and aprons that cannot be easily repaired. Piano and synthetic finishes are almost impossible to repair. Look for peeling, cracks in the wood beneath the finish, or chips in any laminate or vinyl, especially along the feather strip edge and where the pockets are attached. Rail damage detracts greatly from the value of the table and often is expensive or impossible to repair, but, if you're selling, it should be done if at all possible.

Buyer Tip

Look for peeling, cracks, or chips in any laminate or vinyl, especially along the feather strip edge and where the pockets are attached.

Check the finish. Is it smooth and polished, or is it rough, grainy, and dull? Well made tables can be finished to the quality of other expensive furnishings.

Rails take an enormous amount of abuse—cues banging and sliding across them, players leaning and sitting on them, wayward balls bouncing and rolling over them—so if they aren't made with the highest quality finish or highest grade laminates over the hardest of hardwoods, don't expect to pay or receive top dollar.

On the cabinet, legs, and pedestals look for a smooth finish without scratches or gouges, and cracks or potential joint separation. If the table is used, look for water damage; especially pet "water." Yuck. Particle board rails, frames, and legs swell out of shape with a little moisture and simply disintegrate when

Seller Tip
Rail damage detracts greatly from the value of the table and often is expensive or impossible to repair, but it should be done if at all possible.

soaked. Water or any moisture doesn't help
hardwoods either, so look for its presence.

Legs, pedestals, and aprons should be finished
to the same degree of quality as the cabinet and
rails.

Rank the quality of a pool table's finish in the
following order:

Ideal:	1. Piano finish.
	2. Slick lacquer or polyurethane finish.
Good:	Top-quality wood laminate with good, smooth lacquer or polyurethane finish.
Okay:	Top-quality plastic laminate like Formica. Scratch and burn resistant is a plus.
Poor:	1. Synthetic wood grain finish.
	2. Paper-thin wood grain vinyl.

Words of Experience

The first billiard table I re-covered professionally was in the summer of '72, not far from Santa Claus, Indiana. It didn't take the whole summer, but after six hours, I was beginning to think it was going to. At that time, there were no re-covering instructions available, and, as it still is today, no one willing to show you how. If you've never re-covered a rail, the simple things that need to be done to get a professional looking job are almost insurmountable. But, like magic, as bewildering and baffling as it first seems, it becomes obvious once you know the tricks.

The chubby old guy for whom I was working had a bushy white beard, button nose, and small round-rimmed glasses that exaggerated the twinkle in his eyes. While he sat with extreme patience for the time it took me to finish the job, I teased him about being Santa Claus. He, however, insisted that he was not.

On the way home that evening, less than a mile from his house, I saw several deer grazing on the green grass along a creek bank. I counted eight.

Because the coincidences were so humorous, I told my young daughters that I had worked on Santa Claus's table. They, of course, loved the story and insisted that I take them to visit him before the coming Christmas. During that visit, he was wonderfully kind and gracious to the girls. They loved him.

You never know whom you're going to meet in this business.

Words of Experience

Last week, I delivered a table that someone had paid a thousand dollars too much for.

When I delivered it, I said: "You know there's a book available that explains the differences between tables that would've saved you hundreds of dollars."

His answer: "I didn't want to spend the twenty-five bucks.

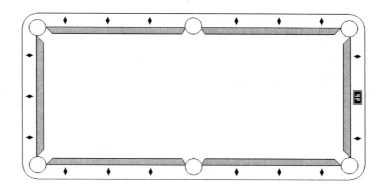

Chapter 7. Cushions

Although cushions and their quality are extremely important to the game of pool, they are not on top of the list of components to consider when buying or selling a table because they are replaceable. But that doesn't mean that they shouldn't be discussed.

Cushions usually deteriorate slowly, and noticing the gradual loss of resiliency of the rubber is impossible while using a particular table

exclusively. Some cushions can last thirty years or
more and still be playable. Normally, however,
they should be replaced every five or six years or
whenever they fail to rebound properly.

Some cushions become hard as they age, and
others will soften, so feeling or squeezing them
won't necessarily give a good indication of their
playability. A better way to determine the amount
of cushion deterioration is to swiftly roll a ball
against a rail. The ball should rebound back and
forth—not around the table—four or five times;
that is, two or three on the first side, and at least
two on the other side (Figure 7-1). Five rebounds
is excellent, four is very good, but anything less is
unsatisfactory.

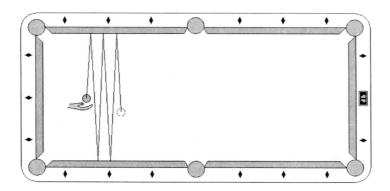

Figure 7-1 *Five rebounds*

Because of distance, a slight difference between end-to-end and side-to-side may be detected, but that should be less than one rebound.

Quality cushions are molded from 100 percent pure gum rubber. Some cheaper cushions are extruded rubber or synthetics, or molded rubber diluted with fillers.

The two most common cushions are the triangular shaped K-66 and U-23 (Figure 7-2).

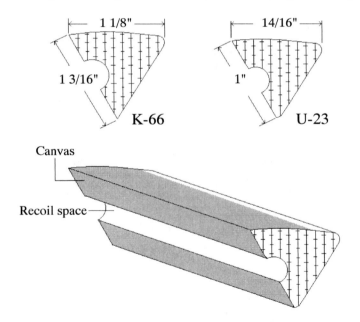

Figure 7-2 *Gum rubber cushions*

Less common cushions are K-55 and #79. K-55 is used on some coin-op and home-style tables, while #79 is used for carom tables. K-66 profile is a high-speed cushion used on most commercial and home-style tables. U-23 profile is a medium speed rubber and is used on most coin-operated, and some home-style tables.

Although these two cushion types may look the same, they can be distinguished by their size. K-66 is $1^3/_{16}$ inches high by $1^1/_8$ inches wide (back to nose), and U-23 is 1 inch high by $^{14}/_{16}$ inch wide.

The critical dimension of a cushion is the height of its nose above the playing surface. The cushion nose is that part of the cushion that makes contact with the ball.

If the cushion nose is too high, the ball will be forced down onto the slate making the rebound dull and slow. If the cushion nose is too low, the ball will be propelled up causing it to hop as it rebounds.

Cushion nose height is determined according to the game ball size. Most rails using full profile cushions have dimensions similar to those in Figure 7-3.

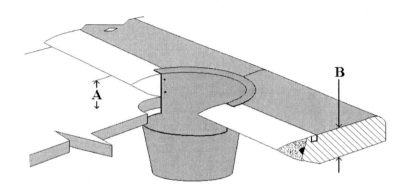

	Pool	Snooker	Carom
(A)	$1^{13}/_{32}$	$1^{21}/_{64}$	$1^{31}/_{64}$
(B)	$1^{1}/_{2}$	$1^{1}/_{2}$	$1^{1}/_{2}$
Ball	$2^{1}/_{4}$	$2^{1}/_{8}$	$2^{3}/_{8}$

Figure 7-3 *Cushion height and rail thickness*

CONCLUSION

Without removing the rail cloth, it isn't always possible to determine what kind of cushions are on a table. However, if the rails are well made, from solid hardwood, they will generally have full profile cushions. If they are cheaply made, from softwoods, particle board, or fiber board,

Buyer Tip

Check the cushions for rebound, and look at all six, not just one or two. They should send a ball four or five times across the table.

physically and visually check the cushions, they could be anything. Non-conforming cushions does not mean the table will not play well, it simply means that the table will not be regulation by any regulatory boards, and that replacement cushions may be hard to come by. Tables equipped with a non-gum and non-conforming profile rubber should be re-cushioned with their specific rubber. The availability of such rubber depends on the age of the table and the manufacturer.

Furthermore, be aware that nonstandard cushions cannot be retrofitted with full profile cushions without major rail reworking to re-cut the angle of the rail to accept either U-23 or K-66 profiles.

Check the cushions for rebound, and look at all six, not just one or two. Are they responsive? They should send a ball four or five times across the table. When the ball hits the cushion, does it sound solid? Ideally, the only sound you should hear is the ball

Seller Tip

If you want top dollar for your table, consider replacing dead rubber.

rolling. Hollow sounds or vibration noises are usually caused by one of three things: Rails that are attached to the frame instead of the slate. Rails not attached solidly to the slate because they are loose or don't have enough rail bolts. Or, the cushion rubber itself is loose. If you get a thud and no rebound, the rubber is dead.

If you're a seller and you want top dollar for your table, consider replacing dead rubber. At least make sure the rail bolts are tight. If the cushions must be replaced, they're not extremely expensive, but it does take time.

For buyers, if the rest of the table is worth purchasing, don't let poor cushions stand in the way, but be prepared to have them changed. It's not something that can be put off.

Also, when the cushions are replaced, the cloth will usually have to be changed—another added expense.

Rank a table's cushions in the follow order:

Ideal: K-66, 100° gum rubber (K-66 or #79 for carom). Four or five rebounds with a no-vibrating, solid sound.

Good: Any other full profile gum rubber, like K-55, U-23, etc. Four or five rebounds with a no-vibrating, solid sound.

Okay: Any profile like K-66 with less
               than 100° gum rubber. Some
               vibrating sounds can be
               tolerated as long as there are at
               least four rebounds.

Poor: Any non-gum, non-standard
               rubber. Any loose or
               improperly aligned cushion
               rubber. Any soft or hard non-
               responsive rubber.

Words of Experience

A few months ago, I got a phone call from a guy who insisted that he "stole" a pool table for six hundred bucks at a garage sale because the owner was moving. He said it was a massive antique, solid oak table, and he wanted me to move it for him.

The table was massive looking all right, but it was just a standard 8-foot, one-piece slate table with leather pockets and a laminated particle board frame. It was not an antique, nor was it solid oak.

On top of the moving charge, the table needed new cushions, new cloth, and new pockets. His steal became a huge dark-brown, pink elephant. He had more money in a used table than it was selling for new.

Beware and be aware.

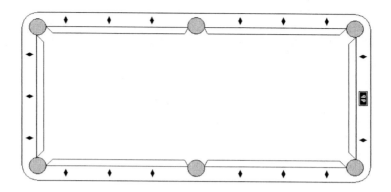

Chapter 8. Pockets

Standard pool and snooker tables have two kinds of ball retrieval systems. One, of course, is six individual pockets that trap the balls in six different locations around the table. The other is a return system in which the balls are returned to a ball collection box at the end or side of the table.

Pockets are either exposed leather (could be plastic or synthetic) with leather or knitted webbing, or are molded leather, rubber, or plastic mounted on the inside or interior of the rail (Figure 8-1).

A ball-return system consists of pocket liners, gully boots, and gully return tracks, all mounted on the interior of the table.

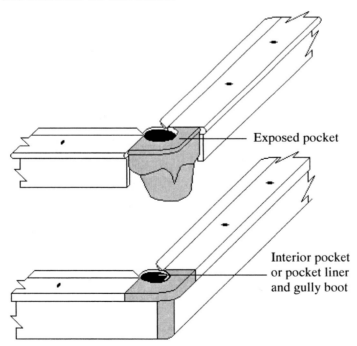

Figure 8-1 *Exposed or interior pockets*

KNIT POCKETS

Knit pockets are rare, found mostly on antique snooker tables, but they can be on any table and are still available. The only difference between a knitted pocket and a leather pocket is the webbing—one is knitted from a heavy twine and the other is cut from leather.

LEATHER POCKETS

Although some leather pockets are molded to fit inside a boxed rail assembly like rubber or plastic pockets, most are made to hang on the outside of the table (Figure 8-2). They become an aesthetic part of the table, an enhancement of its overall charm or beauty. Attractive hand-tooled leathers, died in various pastel colors with fringe trimmings to match, and inlaid with suede, snake skins, imitation animal skins, and pool table cloth, are designed to coordinate the table with any room decor. Leather pockets are more handsome today then ever.

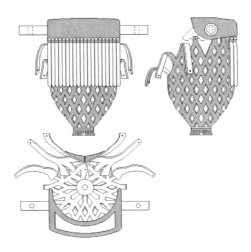

Figure 8-2 *Leather pocket*

Each leather (or knit) pocket consists of five parts: top leather, iron, inside trim, fringe tassel (or leather shield), and webbing (Figure 8-3).

The top leather is formed onto the U-shaped irons to make the upper portion of the pocket. The webbing is sewn or riveted onto the top leather beneath the iron. Inside trim sheathing covers the rivets on the inside, and tassels do the same for the outside. The webbing connects to the table by tabs that are part of the top of the webbing.

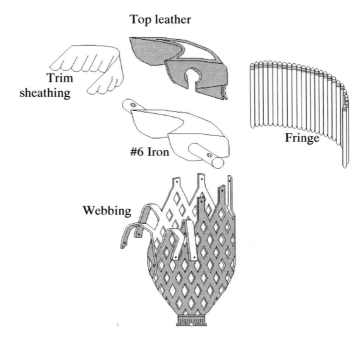

Figure 8-3 *Leather pocket components*

Some inexpensive tables are equipped with plastic or "synthetic leather" in place of real leather, and it's often hard to tell the difference once the trim sheathing and fringe is attached. Close attention is warranted.

Pocket irons are normally cast from iron or aluminum, but some cheaper versions are now

being made from plastic. Lugs that attach the
pocket to the rail are part of the casting. The two
most common irons are the #6 and #3 (Figure 8-4).

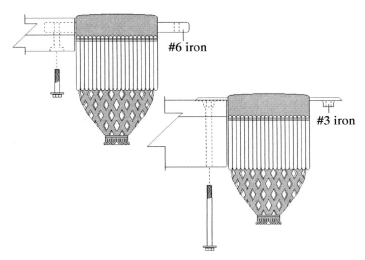

Figure 8-4 *Leather pocket irons*

The lugs of #6 pocket irons insert into holes at
the end of each rail so they are hidden, inside the
rail. The lugs of #3 irons are exposed at the top of
the rail and are chromed or brass plated. Lugs are
drilled and tapped so they can be attached by bolts
that penetrate the rail from the bottom.

MOLDED POCKETS, POCKET LINERS, AND GULLY BOOTS

Most molded pockets and pocket liners are made of plastic or rubber (Figure 8-5) and, on occasion, molded leather. Rubber seems to hold up better than plastic, and of course leather will outperform both plastic and rubber. However, three of four sets of plastic pockets can be replaced at a cost less than one set of leather pockets.

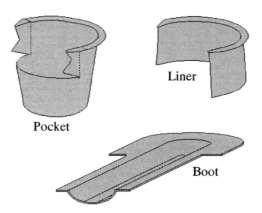

Figure 8-5 *Pocket, liner, boot*

Pocket liners serve the same function as the top portion of the molded pocket. It trims the exposed raw wood of the rail and stapled rail cloth, and, simultaneously, directs the ball down into the pocket, or, with pocket liners, down onto the gully boot and ball-return tracks.

Pocket boots are also plastic or rubber and are used with pocket liners (Figure 8-6). Their function is to quietly direct the ball to the ball return tracks.

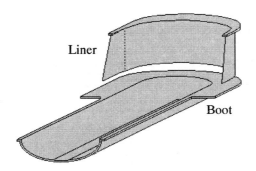

Figure 8-6 *Boot and liner*

GULLIES (BALL RETURNS)

A gully return is a system of tubes or tracks that returns all pocketed balls to a collection box at the end of the table, or to the side of most coin-operated tables. A variety of materials including wood, plastic and cardboard tubes, fiberglass, and plastic coated wire are used for gully returns (Figure 8-7).

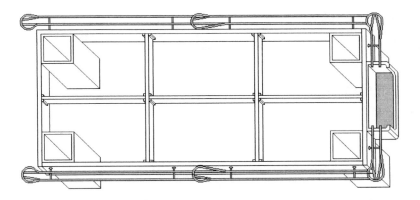

Figure 8-7 *Wire gully system*

All gully systems have one inherent problem: trash. Napkins, cubes of chalk, pencils, tennis balls, stogies, children's toys, cue bumpers, light bulbs, ashtrays—anything that can fit into the pocket can plug it up. The debris can normally be fished out through the pocket or from beneath the table, but occasionally the table must be dismantled to get to it.

CONCLUSION

Which is better, a table with pockets or one with a ball gully system? Of course, it depends on the quality of each, but it really comes down to personal preference because there are no regulations that govern them. The question becomes, do you mind retrieving the balls, or do you want them all in one spot? It's up to you, if you are buying. If you are selling, you don't have to worry about your table being inferior because it is one or the other.

But, whichever it is, carefully check the pockets, liners, boots, or ball gullies to determine if they are in serviceable shape, or if any of them need to be replaced. These are the most overlooked and neglected parts on a pool table.

Leather pockets should be checked to insure the leather webbing has not dried to the point of becoming brittle and ripped. Also, check the area of the pocket that the balls strike (the inside back). After

Buyer Tip

Leather pockets are the most overlooked and neglected parts on a pool table. They should be checked to insure the leather webbing has not dried to the point of becoming brittle and ripped.

extensive use the leather at that point will tear, exposing the pocket iron. The irons themselves, especially cast aluminum and plastic, can be easily broken at the center of the pocket. Since the iron is covered with leather, these breaks cannot be seen. They can, however, be felt by simply holding each pocket at the middle and moving it up and down.

Also—and this is particularly important with the very common #6 irons, and especially on used tables—check the space between the top leather and the top rail, where the pocket and rail butts together. If there's a gap, or if the pocket is hanging loose, maybe the pocket screws need to be tightened. But, more than likely, the bottom of the rail base is broken, allowing the pocket to slump and pull away from the rail. This can be repaired, but it's time consuming and expensive. If it's a priceless antique table, it's worth the effort. Otherwise, the rail base was probably made of some softwood, or particle or fiber board, which simply can't hold up. The only way to know for sure is to take a rail off the table and look. Brand named tables aren't impervious to these short-comings.

If the pockets are tight, with no gaps between the rails and pockets, the rails are probable fine.

The leather pockets themselves, as a percentage of the overall value of a good table, are inexpensive. Conversely, on a cheap table, leather pockets might be the most expensive part of the table. Examine carefully.

   Plastic pockets and pocket liners can also tear at the point where they are struck by the balls, but those *are* inexpensive and should not weigh heavily, if at all, on any buy or sell decision.

   Gully boots and ball gullies should also be checked, but should not figure much into the buying or selling decision, either. They can be replaced with pockets bypassing a bad gully system

Seller Tip

Gullies can be replaced with pockets bypassing a bad gully system altogether if necessary.

altogether if necessary. And, ball gully systems should be checked thoroughly. If they are ineffective from the beginning, they will always be trouble.

Rank a pocket or gully system in the following order:

Pockets:

Ideal:	Leather, exposed or enclosed.
Good:	Synthetic leather, exposed or enclosed.
Okay:	Enclosed plastic.
Poor:	Exposed plastic (in place of leather).

Ball gully:

Ideal:	Coated wire gully.
Good:	Fiberglass gully.
Okay:	Plastic gully (when it works).
Poor:	Wood gully.

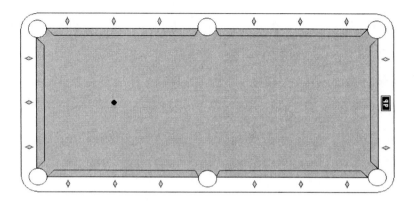

Chapter 9. Cloth

No matter what anyone calls it in normal conversation, pool table cloth is not felt. Felt is a matted fabric of wool or hair or fur fibers adhered together by heat, moisture, and pressure. Pool table (billiard) cloth is a woven blending of nylon and wool, usually at a ratio of 20 or 25 percent nylon, and 80 or 75 percent wool, respectively, or 100 percent wool.

Cloth is also categorized by weight, and sometimes nap. Weight is from 17 to 22 ounce per square foot. Cloth with heavy nap plays slow, and worsted cloth with thin nap plays fast.

Standard pool table cloth will be either directional or non-directional. Directional cloth is so named because the nap lies in one direction, head to foot. Non-directional cloth has nap that lies in random directions. Some cloth has a rubber or canvas backing material bonded to its underside.

Pool table cloth is available in more than thirty different colors and blends. Most colors are included in Table 9-1.

Aztec	Black	Blue
Electric blue	Denver blue	Brown
Burgundy	Camel	Charcoal
Copper	Coral	Canadian
Evergreen	Dark green	Green
Gold	Gray brown	Grape
Lavender	Mahogany	Mauve
Mustard	Orange	Pewter
Purple	Red	Rose
Rust	Sea foam	Spruce
Surf	Taupe	Teal

Table 9-1 *Common cloth colors*

Cloth colors are constantly being changed and updated to stay in step with modern home decor. Also available are a few multicolored designer cloth made by weaving together different colored threads.

Furthermore, as if more than thirty colors are not enough, tables can be covered in two-tone combinations; that is, the cushions one color and the bed cloth another. Some possible combinations: red bed with navy cushions, copper bed with camel cushions, black bed with gray cushions, navy bed with electric blue cushions, mauve bed with surf cushions (very southwestern). Combinations for sport's colors, like purple and orange for the Phoenix Suns basketball team, or navy and gray for the Dallas Cowboys football team, for example, are also possible. Of course, these colors can be reversed, and the combinations are limited only by imagination and taste.

CONCLUSION

It's hard to tell what weight cloth is on a table, but reputable dealers use only high weight, good blend cloth. Cheaper or department store tables are usually covered with the thinnest grade material possible and still be called cloth. But, still, if the table is in reasonable shape, the cloth shouldn't be a deciding buy, sell factor.

Buyer Tip

If the cloth is in good condition, and is a color you like, consider it a bonus because it should have nothing to do with the decision to purchase or reject a good table.

From the seller's standpoint, new cloth alone can make an old table appear new and taken care of, and add to its perceived value.

Seller Tip

New cloth alone can make an old table appear new and taken care of, and add to its perceived value.

Rank the cloth in the following order:

Ideal: 21/22 ounce worsted cloth with
                a wool and nylon blend, or
                100° wool.

Good: 21/22 ounce nap cloth with a
                wool and nylon blend, or 100°
                wool.

Okay: 19/20 ounce wool and nylon
                blend or 100° wool cloth.

Poor: Non-wool cloth, marine vinyl,
                etc.

Words of Experience

Although its size is not godly, Camelback Mountain pushes out of the "Valley of The Sun" like the hump of a camel, lording over the vastness of the cities below. I can stand on the hump, at the summit, pivot three hundred and sixty degrees and take in the panoramic vista of downtown Phoenix to the southwest, Glendale and Peoria to the west, Cave Creek and Carefree to the north, Superstition Mountain and Apache Junction to the east, Mesa and Tempe to the South, and Paradise Valley and Scottsdale beneath me.

The climb from Echo Canyon takes roughly an hour, and is strenuous. Still, for me, the view is well worth the effort. From there, I can see the valley in which I now work. From one end to the other, a hundred miles in every direction, I can see it in one sweeping motion. I crisscross this enormous arroyo every day in pursuit of the thousands of pool tables down there.

I have traveled from Barry Goldwater's nine-foot antique exposed frame table, with hand carved aprons, legs, and pockets sitting in the Wrigley Mansion, to a rancher's more common board and slat frame table sitting in a bunkhouse in Queen Creek. I have traveled from the hundreds of classic tables in mobile home parks around Apache Junction, to a retiree's uni-cabinet, uni-rail table in Sun City. I have traveled from a thousand standard and nonstandard tables in residences and apartment complexes, to a hundred coin-operated bar tables. I have worked on them all.

It's an awesome feeling.

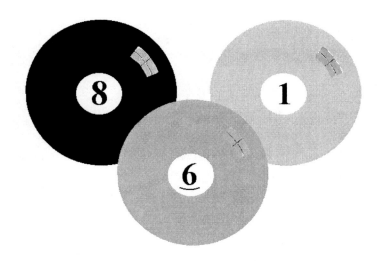

Chapter 10. Accessories

Accessories—balls, brushes, cue racks, etc.—are the last components to consider when buying or selling a table. Generally, if a table isn't worth the money without the accessories, it isn't worth the money with them. There are exceptions, of course. If the table is worth, say, a thousand

dollars, and the seller wants to throw in an eight
hundred dollar cue or light fixture, then by all
means factor in the accessories. But remember, if
the accessories cost as much as the table, the table
can't be very good. Lights, cues, and to a lesser
degree, balls, have such a disparity in quality and
price that often they should be dealt with separately
and not as part of a pool table deal.

LIGHTS

Traditional pool table lights hang above the
table, are supported from the ceiling by chains or
cords, and come in many shapes and sizes (Figure
10-1).

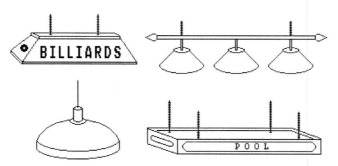

Figure 10-1 *Light fixtures*

Hanging lights are usually decorative, and add ambience to the poolroom. Fixtures with two or more incandescent lamps are superior to a single lamp simply because they distribute light more evenly across the table. However, whether one lamp or more, incandescent lights tend to cast distracting darkish shadows of the balls, cue, and player's hand.

Although some unavoidable light shadowing might still exist, good fluorescent lights eliminate most of the bothersome shadows caused by incandescent lamps. Fluorescent fixtures that hang, though, are usually long and boxy, and not very attractive. But those that are attached directly to or recessed into the ceiling (although adding nothing to ambience) create a room that is bright, pleasant, and virtually without shadows.

Hanging Light Clearance

There are no set rules on the height of a hanging light above the playing surface of a pool table, but eye level is usually accepted. A good rule-of-thumb, though, since eye level varies with each person, is to place the lower rim of the fixture about 3 feet above the table (Figure 10-2), or $5^1/_2$

feet from the floor. It is also a good idea to have the bottom edge of the fixture slightly below eye level so it is low enough to prevent eyestrain, yet high enough to be out of the way of play.

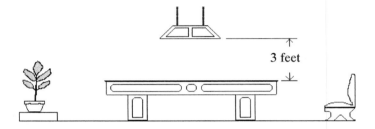

Figure 10-2 *Clearance above table*

An overriding factor, however, is that the fixture should evenly distribute light over the entire playing surface. If at 3 feet only the middle of the table is illuminated, the fixture should be raised. If light floods over the edge of the table, the fixture should be lowered.

Moreover, the lamp should be powerful enough to evenly distribute bright, but not glaring, light over the entire playing surface without deviating more than a few inches from the 3-foot height level. Three 60-watt bulbs or two 4-foot fluorescent tubes should do it.

Large fixtures that approach the width or length of the table should be hung high enough to prevent players from bumping their heads when playing.

Light fixtures range from cheap plastic to ultra expensive cut and beveled glass, from giveaway promotional beer fixtures to priceless collectable giveaway promotional beer fixtures.

CUES

A pool cue can be junk or an expensive and personal accessory, ranging from throwaway to sentimentally overpriced, and is generally of higher interest to a potential buyer or seller than are the other accessories. For that reason, I have chosen to cover them in greater detail than the other accessories.

Cues are made as either one piece, or two pieces that are joined when playing. Cues made in more than two pieces are not generally considered good quality or well made.

One-piece Cues

Good quality one-piece (house) cues are actually made from two pieces of wood. Maple is used for the shaft and rosewood, mahogany, maple, or some other hardwood for the butt. The two pieces are bonded together normally using a four-prong joint, but could have a flat face joint with the two halves pinned together (Figure 10-3).

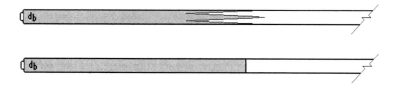

Figure 10-3 *One-piece cues*

The use of two pieces of wood is for more than decoration. Maple is used on the shaft for its hardness and trueness; while heavier woods are used for the butt to control the cue's weight distribution. Often, though, metal plugs or screws are inserted into the butt for added weight.

High quality one-piece cues are excellent, inexpensive cues. They are well balanced, sized, and properly weighted.

Low quality one-piece cues are usually made from one piece of inferior wood with the four prongs painted on. They are often too light and improperly balanced for good play.

One-piece cues are also made from graphite, fiberglass, aluminum, and other non-wood materials.

Even the best quality one-piece cues, though, are inexpensive in relation to the price of a pool table.

Two-piece Cues

The nomenclature used to describe a pool cue may differ somewhat depending on the area, manufacturer, and cost. However, those depicted in the following drawing are adequate to allow a thorough understanding of most cues (Figure 10-4).

Two-piece cues are made from a variety of materials: fiberglass, aluminum, graphite, plastic sheathed wood, etc. Still, whether one-piece house cues or two-piece custom cues, the better cues are made from wood alone.

Non-wood materials have come a long way in their ability to impart english on a cue ball, and the simple fact that they will not warp is a major advancement over wood. Still, the feel, consistent control, and beauty of wood cannot be duplicated

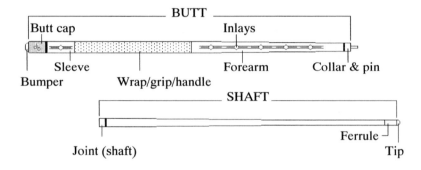

Figure 10-4 *Standard 2-piece cue*

Shafts

Although other materials and woods are employed to manufacture cue shifts, maple is by far the most frequently used, and Canadian maple is considered the best. Canadian maple, rock maple, and hard maple are different names given to the same sugar maple wood. Sugar maple is extremely dense, with a tight straight grain, and is excellent for cue shafts.

Maple trees are logged in the coldest winter months while the tree is in hibernation and the sap is in the roots to insure the driest possible wood. The tree is sawed into planks, which are allowed to air dry for several months before they are put in a kiln. After drying, the planks are cut into rough shafts, usually octagons, then allowed to dry for another six to twelve months before being turned on a lathe.

Top quality shafts are always pro-tapered to give them the same diameter from the cue tips back 10 to 12 inches toward the joints (Figure 10-5). This helps create a solid level stroke as the cue slides through a bridge.

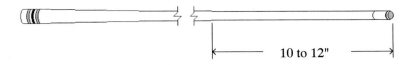

10 to 12"

Figure 10-5 *Pro-taper*

The diameters of shafts at the tips and along the pro-tapers range from 11 to 14 millimeters. The ideal cue shaft size is said to be between 12 and 13 millimeters ($^1/_2$ inch). The real size criterion, however, is that a shaft should fit comfortably within a player's hand.

Joints

A two-piece cue shaft is mechanically attached to the butt by a joint. There are four basic kinds of cue joints: double screw, single screw, implex, and quick release.

1. A double screw joint is a double metal screw that turns into a double metal pin. Both halves of the joint (collars) are metal, usually stainless steel, so that the joining face is metal to metal. The double screws, arranged one inside the other, makes an extremely stiff joint (joint 1 in Figure 10-6).

2. A single screw joint is a metal screw that turns into a metal threaded insert. The two halves of the joint are metal and metal, plastic and metal, or plastic and plastic, with the metal screw in the center. This joint is stiff to medium stiff (joint 2 in Figure 10-6).

3. An implex joint is a metal screw that screws into a tapped hole in the end of the shaft, either directly into the wood or into a plastic or Lucite insert. The joining face of an implex joint can be plastic to wood, but is usually wood to wood, making this joint the most flexible (joint 3 in Figure 10-6).

4. The quick release is a stainless steel or titanium pin that slips into a retaining insert in the shaft. Two or three quick turns lock the shaft into place. The joining face is metal to plastic or fiber, or wood-to-wood, making the joint medium to flexible in stiffness (joint 4 in Figure 10-6).

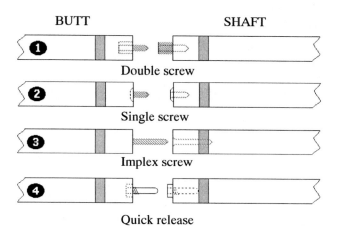

Figure 10-6 *Cue joints*

Butts

The better cue butts are also made of hardwood, or a combination of hardwoods, like ash, maple, and rosewood. Weight is controlled by using woods of different density, or metal plugs or screws inserted into the ends of the butts.

The diameter of a butt ranges from $1^1/_2$ inch to 2 inches. Ultimately, though, butt size is determined by how comfortably it fits the player's hand.

To protect the end of the butt, it is fitted with a high impact plastic butt cap. A rubber bumper is inserted into the butt cap to save furniture and floors.

Depending on what the buyer is willing to spend, the butt area above and below the wrap can be inlaid with an assortment of materials, ranging from plastic to diamonds, including ebony, bone, mother-of-pearl, and dyed hardwoods.

However, inlays are usually not customized individually. Typically, custom cues are ordered by choosing the diameter of the shaft and butt, the weight of the cue, and the color or type of wrap.

The butt will be one of several pre-designed, pre-made, and mass-produced butts, with the inlays already embedded, and the most common of these inlays is mother-of-pearl and colorful hardwoods.

Butts are finished with a clear coat finish to protect the wood while allowing its natural beauty to show.

Wraps

The entire cue butt can be left with exposed wood, but for better grasping, the grip area is usually wrapped in nylon, leather, or Irish linen. Ignoring the player's preference and feel, the only advantage of one wrap over the other is either aesthetic or cost, with nylon being the cheapest (sometimes even cheaper than finished wood), and linen being the most expensive and having the greatest visual appeal.

Cue Tips

Cue tips are merely discs of tanned leather in some variance of compression from soft to hard. Some expensive tips are chemically treated with a finishing polish, compressed and calibrated for hardness. Some are infused with chalk to prevent miscuing, others are simply pressed, stamped leather and are not treated in any fashion. A vinyl or leather base is often bonded to the back of the tip to facilitate adhesion to the ferrule.

Soft tips take chalk better than hard, but hard tips have greater durability. Cuing the ball causes soft tips to compress and conform to the ball's shape, allowing for maximum contact. This makes soft tips more forgiving and less prone to miscuing. Hard tips, on the other hand, will not give or contort when they strike the cue ball. Hard tips must be chalked often, stroked with precision, and the cue ball must be hit closer to center to prevent miscuing.

Ferrules

Ferrules are usually installed onto a tenon cut into the end of the shaft, or onto metal screws that are implanted into the shaft end (Figure 10-7).

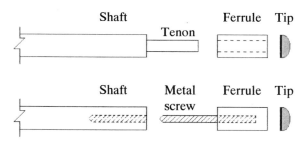

Figure 10-7 *Ferrules*

Ferrules are sleeves or points installed onto the end of the cue shaft to prevent the wood from splitting or splintering. They are made of plastic, fiber, Lucite, or phenolic. Plastic ferrules are used on inexpensive cues, and Lucite or phenolic on higher priced custom cues. Fiber ferrules are generally used on one-piece house cues, but can be found on some inexpensive custom cues.

Size

In general, the weights of cues range from 15 to 22 ounces, with no minimum and 25 ounces deemed the maximum. The best neutral cue weight is between 18 and 20 ounces. Cue weights are determined by an individual's preference, stroke, feel, and experience.

Shaft diameters are measured in millimeters and range between 9 and 14, usually in increments of $^1/_2$ mm.

The length of pool and carom cues is generally considered to be 57 inches, although they can be any length—60, 54, 48, etc., down to 40 inches with no maximum. Snooker cues are usually 60 inches long, and rebound pool cues are 48.

There is no right or wrong weight, length, or size, as long as the player is comfortable using the cue.

BALLS

Originally, pool balls were made of wood, then clay (mud balls), then ivory, and now phenolic resin (thanks to John Wesley Hyatt who invented the resin process for making balls). Because they stay round, are consistent in weight, and are less likely to crack or chip, phenolic balls are far superior to any of the others. At one time ivory cue balls were considered the exception. It was believed that ivory was "alive" and concentrated its energy in the direction of the spin, giving better english. However, ivory balls were laden with natural cracks, easily chipped, and prone to becoming out of round. (Not to mention that only one to three balls could be taken from each elephant's tusk, so the pool table business alone would have made them extinct by now.)

Phenolic balls are made by condensing phenol (usually from coal tar) and an aldehyde to produce a durable resin. The resins are blended in precise amounts to guarantee the correct weight and balance, then cast into balls. The balls go through several baking processes to insure density and cohesion of the inlaid numbers, which cannot peel or wear off (Figure 10-8).

Figure 10-8 *Cutaway 9 ball*

The balls are then ground to a precise spherical diameter and weight, and polished to obtain their vibrant colors and resistance to cloth friction.

The three basic styles of phenolic balls differ in appearance and (supposedly) density. Premium or professional balls have their numbers embedded in the stripe, and non-premium balls have their numbers embedded in the field (middle of the white) of the ball. A third phenolic ball now available has silk-screened stripes and numbers.

The ball itself is good in quality, but the stripes and numbers eventually wear off.

Marbleized or swirled balls are good quality, phenolic balls, and, although fun, are novel and expensive. Clear acrylic balls are also available, but they seem more for show or gimmicks than playing. Also available are inexpensive 4-ounce plastic balls. Plastic balls should be avoided even on an inexpensive table. They do not react properly when striking each other or the cushions. Practicing with these balls can adversely affect a player's game when he or she turns to regulation balls.

Size

A standard phenolic resin pool ball weighs 6 ounces and has a diameter of $2^1/_4$ inches. A traditional set of balls consists of fifteen numbered balls and one cue ball. The cue ball is white, the first eight numbered balls are a solid color, and the remaining seven have colored stripes.
Pool ball colors are shown in Table 10-1.

Non-traditional balls are also available. An excellent example is swirled or marbleized balls that look like they were mixed in a blender. Even these balls, however, adhere to the typical color scheme shown above.

Ball color	Solid number	Striped number
White	Cue ball	- -
Yellow	1 ball	9 ball
Blue	2 ball	10 ball
Red	3 ball	11 ball
Purple	4 ball	12 ball
Orange	5 ball	13 ball
Green	6 ball	14 ball
Burgundy	7 ball	15 ball
Black	8 ball	- -

Table 10-1 *Pool ball colors*

Snooker balls weigh $5^1/_4$ to $5^1/_2$ ounces and have a diameter of $2^1/_8$ inches (the most common), or in some cases $2^1/_{16}$ inches. A set of snooker balls consists of fifteen red balls and six colored balls. Each of the six colored balls has a specific value that is usually, but not always, numbered to reflect that value (Table 10-2).

Ball color	Ball number
Red	(not numbered)
Black	7 ball
Pink	6 ball
Blue	5 ball
Brown	4 ball
Green	3 ball
Yellow	2 ball

Table 10-2 *Snooker ball colors*

Common carom balls weigh $7^1/_4$ ounces each with a diameter of $2^3/_8$ inches. Other acceptable carom balls weigh between 7 and $7^1/_2$-ounces with diameters of $2^{27}/_{64}$ and $2^7/_{16}$ inches. A standard set of carom balls consists of three balls—two white cue balls and one red object ball. One cue ball has a distinguishing mark, usually a small circle or dot.

Rebound pool balls should be $2^1/_8$ inches in diameter and weigh approximately $5^1/_4$ ounces. Although phenolic rebound pool balls are available, inexpensive lightweight 4-ounce plastic balls are the most prevalent.

A set of rebound pool balls consists of two groups of five non-numbered balls. One group is usually red, the other white. The break ball of each group is distinguished by a large dot of the opposite color.

CHALKS

Cue chalk (Figure 10-9) is used to increase friction between the cue tip and the cue ball, virtually eliminating miscues. Chalk is produced from silica, pigmentations for color, and other compounds to hold it together and create density. Chalk's density affects its ability to transfer and stick to the cue tip. The denser the chalk the less likely it is to transfer; the softer, the more it will transfer, to the point of becoming messy.

Cue chalk will also stain cloth and carpet, so using a color that matches both is important.

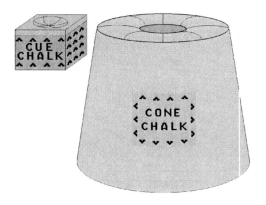

Figure 10-9 *Pool chalks*

A white cone chalk is used to keep a player's hand dry and slick (Figure 10-9). Its usefulness is questionable, and it is extremely messy if not used sparingly.

BRUSHES

There are two kinds of pool table brushes that should be used on cloth (Figure 10-10).

   The common bed cloth brush is used to brush
the playing surface. Quality bed cloth brushes are
approximately ten inches long and have horsehair
bristles. The bristles on the ends are longer than
those in the middle so the brush can be used
beneath the cushion overhang.
   The other brush is strictly for cleaning beneath
the cushion overhang. This brush is handy but not
essential. Because of its plastic bristles, it should be
used sparingly, lightly, and only beneath the
cushion overhang.

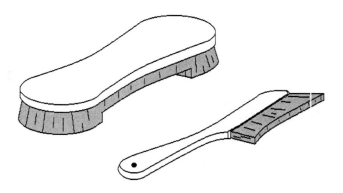

Figure 10-10 *Table brushes*

MECHANICAL BRIDGES

Mechanical bridges (Figure 10-11) are designed for two purposes. One is to allow a player to extend across the table for a shot that could not otherwise be reached. The other is to allow a player to play over a ball that has blocked the cue ball.

Mechanical bridges are usually stored on hooks, within easy reach, beneath one side of the table.

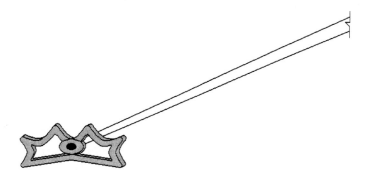

Figure 10-11 Mechanical bridge

GLOVES

Pool gloves are a recent addition to a player's arsenal, and they are as practical as they are gaudy.

Pool gloves cover only the bridge fingers and are made of Polyester or nylon Spandex. They make the player's bridge as slick as powder without the mess. The cue shaft can be clamped tightly within a bridge and still slide with relative ease, eliminating the need for talc, powder, and cue cleaners.

Initially, like most innovations of this type, they were shunned by "fashioned minded" players. But that is changing.

TRIANGLES

Most triangles (or fifteen ball racks) are triangular shaped frames made of plastic or wood used for positioning a set of balls on the playing surface.

Some triangles (ball racks) are made to force the balls into the cloth to insure a tight rack. These racks are more expensive than a standard triangle and aren't really necessary for most home or pool rooms use.

Seven and nine ball racks are usually called diamonds.

DUST COVERS

Dust covers are used to protect the table's bed cloth and top rails from sunlight, pets, spills and thrills, and of course dust. So, when using the table for hobbies, changing baby's diapers, sorting dirty laundry, cleaning the carburetor, and so on, use a cover.

CUE RACKS

Cue racks are designed to store cues in a vertical position to help prevent warping. Cue racks can be mounted to the wall or sat on the floor, depending on design.

Racks can be as simple as two pieces of wood made to hold only six or so cues costing only a few dollars, to something elaborate costing hundreds of dollars that holds ten or twelve cues, balls, accessories, and drinks.

CUE CASES

Cue cases are designed to carry and protect from one to several two-piece cues. They come in a variety of colors with shoulder straps and accessory pouches and pockets.

Soft cases are made of vinyl or soft leather and lined with cotton, foam, velvet, or such material.

Hard cases are made from wood, aluminum, plastic, or leather. They are lined with cloth, wool, velvet, fleece, etc.

Hard cases are generally considered superior to soft cases for storing a cue for long periods or transporting over long distances.

CONCLUSION

There is no reason to play on, or even look at, a cheap table just because it comes with a nice pool cue, light, or

Buyer Tip

There is no reason to look at, a cheap table just because it comes with a nice pool cue or other accessories.

an agglomeration of other accessories. Again, if the

accessory is worth more than the pool table, buy or sell it separately from the table.

And, there are the exceptions, I mentioned before. If the table is worth, say, a thousand dollars, and the seller wants to throw in an eight hundred dollar cue or light fixture, then by all means factor in the accessories. But remember, if the accessories cost as much as the table, the table can't be very good.

Seller Tip

Well maintained, bright and shinny accessories make a mediocre table look present-able

From a sellers standpoint, well maintained, bright and shinny accessories make a mediocre table look presentable, but don't cheapen an expensive table with worthless accessories. And don't over accessorize either, you won't get your money out of the deal. Also, fixtures or cues should never be given away because you feel they should stay with the table, they can and do sell on their own.

Rank the accessories in the following order:

Ideal: New, top-quality accessory package
                that includes four to six brand name
                one-piece cues. Cue rack comparable
                in quality to the table.

                Full set of premiere phenolic balls.
                Wooden triangle. Horsehair brush.
                Chalk to match cloth color.

Good: Two to four brand name one-piece
                cues. Good quality cue rack. Phenolic
                balls. Triangle. Brush. Chalk.

Okay: Two one-piece cues. Cue rack.
                Crown phenolic balls. Plastic triangle.
                Brush. Chalk.

Poor: Cheap one-piece cues.
                Plastic 4-ounce balls.
                Any overused or worn-out
                accessories.

Words Of Experience

The legendary Minnesota Fats came to the grand opening of the Velvet Rail. He was there for two nights of exhibition shooting.

In public Minnesota Fats insisted that he would only shoot for money, and only if the stakes were greater than a thousand a game. But during the hours we spent shaking down the table he was to do his exhibition shooting on, he taught me a great deal about practicing, not only the ten essential shots listed in *A Rookie's Guide to Playing Winning Pool*, but also ball contact, over and under aiming, cloth roll, and of course, hustling. "You never get so good as to not practice these essentials," he told me. "particularly hustling."

Minnesota Fats was a gracious, rotund man with impeccable manners. During performances and public appearances, he insisted on wearing a sports coat and collared shirt, though not usually a tie. But on the road, he sometimes became unrecognizable, often looking quite the bum. If you didn't recognize him in front of a pool room, out of compassion, you might slip him a dollar or two, which he would gladly take, needed or not. And if you gave him a chance on the tables inside, you'd give him the rest of your money, too.

Minnesota Fats was indoctrinated into the BCA hall of fame without winning a major tournament. BCA's reasoning was his lifetime contribution of promoting the game.

He was a master. The game will miss him.

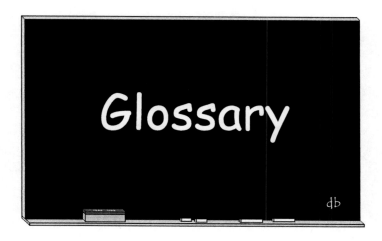

APRONS: A decorative board connected to the side of a rail to hide the edge of the slate, tacking board, and parts of the frame. Aprons are also called blinds, fascia boards, and shields.

BACKED SLATE: Backing boards are attached to the bottom of some slate to help preserve the slate's flatness.

BACKED CLOTH: Some billiard cloth has vinyl adhered to the back or underside to make the cloth rip resistant.

BALK AREA (Kitchen): The area between the head string and the head rail.

BALL BOX: A box that collects the balls from a gully return system.

BCA: Billiard Congress of America. BCA is America's most prominent billiard regulating group.

BED: The part of the table that becomes the playing field once the table is assembled.

BED CLOTH: The pool table cloth attached to the playing field.

BILLIARD CLOTH: A woven fabric made of wool or a blend of wool and nylon. Billiard cloth is also called pool table cloth or fabric.

BILLIARDS: All pool table and pool games including, Carom, Pool (pocket billiards), Snooker, etc. are considered billiards.

BRUSHES: There are two brushed used for pool tables: the bed brush and a brush used for cleaning beneath the rails.

CABINET: The exposed portion of any table.

CAROM: 1. Carom is the deflection of one ball from another ball, or from a cushion. 2. A billiard game in which the table has no pockets and the cue ball is caromed from object balls and cushions.

CLOTH ROLL: A slow rolling ball follows the direction of the lie of the cloth's nap or weaving, making the table appear off level. Often called nap roll.

CUSHION: The rubber attached to the inside of a rail and covered with cloth. The cushion is that part of the rail that rebounds the ball.

CUSHION NOSE: That part of the cushion that contacts the ball.

DIAMOND: 1. One of 18 inlays on the top rail used to aid in shot making. 2. A Nine Ball rack.

ENGLISH: Spin imparted on the cue ball by stroking it off-center.

FACING: Laminated rubber and canvas, or cork attached to the end of the cushions to deaden the ball's rebound.

FEATHER STRIP: A wood or plastic strip that friction-holds the rail cloth into a groove at the top of the rail.

FELT: A matted material that is *not* used on pool tables. Although pool table cloth is often called felt, it is not. See Billiard Cloth.

FERRULE: A sleeve or point installed on the end of a cue shaft to prevent splitting or splintering.

FOOT RAIL: The end rail at the rack end of the table. It is usually the end rail without the nameplate.

FRAME: That portion of a table that gives support to the slate.

FULL SIZE SLATE: A slate that extends beneath the rails, allowing the rails to be fastened securely to the slate.

HEAD RAIL: The end rail at the break end of the table. It is usually the end rail that carries the nameplate.

HOME or HOME-STYLE TABLE: A table made for the home; that is, noncommercial.

JOINT: 1. The connecting collars, pins, and screws that join the pieces of a two-piece cue is the cue joint. 2. The seam of a multi-piece slate set.

LEVELERS: Adjustable leveling pods attached to pool table feet.

MITERED CAPS: Plastic or metal trim that covers the rail ends where they join at the corners.

OVERSIZE SLATE: Slate that extends beneath the rails, allowing the rails to be attached directly and solidly to the slate.

PARALLEL TAPER: See pro-taper.

PLAYING FIELD: 1. The bed cloth. 2. The area designated for game play.

PLAYING SURFACE: 1. The slate, marble, board, etc. that the bed cloth is attached to.

POOL: A common name given to billiard games in general, and pocket billiards in particular.

PRO-TAPER: The narrow end of a cue shaft that has the same diameter as the tip, extending backwards eight to ten inches.

RACK: 1. The triangular-shaped frame used to position the balls. 2. The balls themselves after the triangle has been removed. 3. Any device that holds the cues.

RAIL CASTINGS: Metal castings that join the rails to each other.

RAIL CLOTH: The billiard cloth attached to the rails.

RE-COVER: The installation of new cloth.

REGULATION: Regulations are rules set by regulating bodies like the Billiard Congress of America (BCA). A regulation pool table, for example, is what the regulating body determines it to be for a given tournament; it is not necessarily a nine-foot table.

SCRATCH: A foul shot in which the cue ball leaves the playing surface.

SEAM: The connection joints of a multi-piece slate set.

SHIM: Flat or tapered stock used to level a pool table.

SLATE PLATFORM: A stiff, flat, and solid board surface at the top of a cabinet or frame that serves as a bed for the slate.

SNOOKER: A pool game played on a large table with six pockets, fifteen red balls, and six numbered balls.

STANDARD SIZE SLATE: Slate that ends beneath the cushion but still allows the rails to be attached to the slate, usually from the side.

TACKING BOARD: A board affixed to the bottom of the slate to provide a means of attaching the cloth.

TACKING STRIP: The bottom portion of the rail used to attach the rail cloth to the rail.

UNDERSIZE SLATE: A slate that ends at the inner edge of the rails, usually beneath the cushion. The rails are attached to the frame and not the slate itself.

UNBACKED SLATE: Some slate is just slabs of rock with no backing. The slate is laid directly onto the slate platform, which may or may not double as a means of cloth attachment. Usually the cloth is glued to the slat.

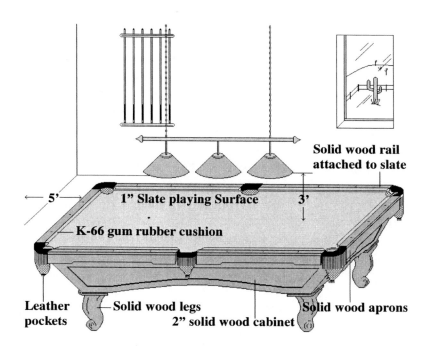

Solid wood rail attached to slate

← 5' →

1" Slate playing Surface   **3'**

K-66 gum rubber cushion

Leather pockets   **Solid wood legs**   **Solid wood aprons**

2" solid wood cabinet

Quick Reference Specifications for an Ideal Table and Room

POOL ROOM

Ideal: 10 feet wider and 10 feet longer than the pool table size (5 feet clearance), with no obstructions.

Accept: 9 feet wider and 9 feet longer than the pool table ($4^1/_2$ feet clearance), with no obstructions.

Pass on: Any room small enough to force a player to raise the butt of his or her cue for any shot, including a rail shot, is simply too small.

TABLE

Ideal: Any established manufacturers' pro-line or high-end table as long as it meets the ideal criteria of this list.

Accept: Established manufacturers' mid-range or low-end table, as long as it meets the acceptable criteria of this list.

Pass on: Department store, non-slate (particle board, fiber board, honey comb, etc.), or any other table *not* meeting the ideal or acceptable criteria of this list.

RAILS

Ideal: Solid hardwood rails attached to the slate by bolts and inserted lug nuts or nut plates, with solidly affixed wood aprons. A four-bolt pattern on 8-foot or larger tables is a plus.

Accept: Solid hardwood rails attached to the slate by bolts and inserted lug nuts or nut plates, with solidly affixed non-wood aprons.

Pass on: Any particle board or other non-wood rail. Any rail *not* firmly and solidly attached to the slate. Any rail attached with screws or lag bolts.

PLAYING SURFACE

Ideal: 1 inch or thicker, three-piece standard or oversize slate, backed, and $29^1/_4$ to 31 inches above the floor with $29^1/_2$ inches recommended.

Accept: $^3/_4$ inch or thicker (preferably backed) three-piece oversize slate.

Pass on: Any undersize slate, either one- or three-piece. Any non-slate playing surface—particle board, honeycomb, fiber board, slateen, slatron, etc.

PLAYING FIELD

Ideal: Any of the following standard sizes.

Table size	Field size
6 x 12	68 x 136
5 x 10	56 x 112
$4^1/_2$ x 9	50 x 100
4 x 8 os	46 x 92
4 x 8	44 x 88
$3^1/_2$ x 7	38 x 78

Accept: 3 x 6 (34 x 68) or any small table, as long as it is twice as long as it is wide.

Pass on: Any non-standard dimension table, especially one that is not twice as long as it is wide.

FRAME/CABINET

Ideal: All hardwood constructed frame or cabinet that is rigid, allowing no side to side or end to end movement.

Accept: Any non-wood frame (such as steel) that is rigid, allowing no side to side or end to end movement.

Pass on: Any particle board or other non-wood frame or cabinet.

LEGS/PEDESTALS

Ideal: All wood, rigid, and attached solidly to the frame, frame member, or cabinet, allowing no side to side or end to end movement.

Accept: Any non-wood leg or pedestal (such as steel) that is rigid, allowing no side to side or end to end movement.

Pass on: Any particle board or other non-wood leg or pedestal. Any leg attached to the frame by metal corner brackets.

FINISH

Ideal: Wood polished to a hard, smooth, and durable finish. Rail sights should be flush and smooth.

Accept: Some laminates such a Formica, that is mar, scratch and burn resistant. Rail sights should be flush and smooth.

Pass on: Any thin plastic laminates or synthetic wood grain finishes, etc. Any rail system that has rough, raised, painted, ink screened, or unfinished sights.

CUSHIONS

Ideal: Full K-66 profile, 100% gum rubber cushions that are set at a height of $1^{13}/_{32}$ for a pool table, $1^{21}/_{64}$ for snooker, and $1^{31}/_{64}$ for carom.

Accept: Gum rubber K-55 or U-23 profile, set at the proper height.

Pass on: Any non-standard profile or material.

POCKETS

Ideal: Interior or exposed leather pockets that are 4 inches round with a $4^{7}/_{8}$ to $5^{1}/_{8}$ corner pocket and $5^{3}/_{8}$ to $5^{5}/_{8}$ center pocket opening for pool tables, and $3^{1}/_{2}$ inches round with a $3^{3}/_{8}$ to $3^{5}/_{8}$ corner pocket and $4^{1}/_{16}$ to $4^{5}/_{16}$ center pocket opening for snooker. Gully returns (if you must) that are coated

wire, fiberglass, or similar material
that are quiet and clog-proof.

Accept: Interior pockets or pocket liners made
of quality plastic or rubber on gully
return tables. Gullies must be made of
coated wire, fiberglass, or similar
material that are quiet and clog-proof.

Pass on: Exterior plastic pockets, even those
called "synthetic leather." Plastic or
wood gullies of any kind.

CLOTH

Ideal: 100% wool, or a woven blend of 75%
worsted wool and 25% nylon fabric,
weighing 21 to 22 ounces or greater.

Accept: 100% wool, or a woven blend of 75%
worsted wool and 25% nylon fabric,
weighing 19 to 20 ounces.

Pass on: Any blend fabric weighing less than
19 ounces. Any non-wool cloth, felt,
marine vinyl, Naugahyde, etc.

ACCESSORIES

Ideal: Fluorescent light at a height of approximately three feet.

        Balls weigh 6 ounces and have a $2^1/_4$ inch diameter for pool, weigh $5^1/_2$ ounces and have a $2^1/_8$ inch diameter for snooker, and weigh $7^1/_4$ ounces and have a $2^3/_8$ inch diameter for carom.

        Standard cues are 57 inches long for pool and 60 inches long for snooker. Two-piece cues should be pro-tapered.

Accept: Incandescent light or lights at a height of approximately three feet. Other accessories should be the same as above.

Pass on: Cheap one-piece cues. Plastic or acrylic 4 ounce balls. Any overused or worn-out accessory.

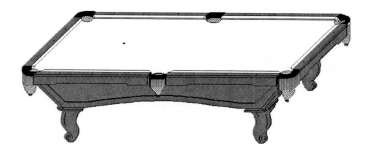

Table Ranking

I derived at this ranking by using most of the components of this book—rails, playing surface, frames and cabinets, legs and pedestals, finish, cushions, and pockets—and I put no weight on table condition or age, but assume the tables are new or in a like-new state. This ranking reflects value only in that any table should be worth more than a table ranked below it, because of the materials or craftsmanship used in manufacturing. Also, this ranking is not intended to reflect on or draw conclusions as to the ethics or standards of any manufacturer, distributor, or retailer. It's only purpose is to give an impartial judgment to the manner and quality of construction of a sampling of various tables available to a potential buyer or seller, and that cannot be done without mentioning brand names and models, which I have listed alphabetically.

A 10 ranking would be given to any perfect table with no manufactured deficiencies of any part of any one of the components listed above, and although several came close, I've yet to find one that I would rank as perfect. Any slight deficiency dropped the ranking to 9. For example, an otherwise perfect table with something as simple as slate screws that loosen or blinds that can pull free easily, or the use some form of laminate or particle board, received a 9 ranking, which is still excellent. Two slight deficiencies or one major manufacturing deficiency dropped the ranking to 8. An example of two slight deficiencies would be particle board blinds and low quality cushions, and a major deficiency would be poor finish, particle board rails, or metal leg mounting brackets. Three deficiencies dropped the ranking to 7, and so on.

Of course there are some tables so poorly constructed that they automatically deserved a 1 ranking. An all particle board or fiber board table—rails, blinds, legs, playing surface (including honeycomb)—is an example of a table that was automatically ranked 1.

If an otherwise inferior table had some quality, like wood rails, for instance, I raised the ranking to 2.

Any undersize slate, with particle or fiber board rails that attach to the frame was automatically ranked 3.

Undersize slate tables made of wood was ranked between 4 and 6, and one-piece slate tables automatically received a 5, or 6 if the cabinets were made of wood.

Because this is a sample, not all tables are listed. If your table isn't listed, find one or two that are similar and rank yours the same. Furthermore, if you have a table that you want ranked in a future revision of this book, or feel that one was not ranked correctly, please send me your information and specifications.

I do not attempt to give a monetary value to any table, new or used, but I normally determine the value of a used table by halving its new cost, then adding upgrades and subtracting damages. There are a couple of exceptions. One: if you bought a new table at an auction or on eBay for $995, don't expect to sell it for that on the used market any time soon, and you'll be lucky to get half of your original investment back. Two: on the other hand, if you bought a $10,000 table from a reputable dealer, you're likely to get as much as three-quarters of your money back on the used market. And, an antique table is, of course, worth whatever you can talk someone into giving you for it, or whatever you can get out of it.

Ranking Index:		
10. Perfect	6. Okay	2. Poor
9. Excellent	5. Playable	1. Inferior
8. Very good	4. Tolerable	
7. Good	3. Mediocre	

ASIAN: Rank 3-5

Asian tables come in a variety of names and styles. They are being sold by major manufactures, often under their own brand name. They are being sold as warehouse, wholesale, truckload, and half-price tables. They are being sold from plush show rooms to storage rooms, including garages, apartments, parking lots (out of the back of trucks), and, of course, they are being sold online, especially eBay. And everyone gives them a different "American" or "wholesale" name.

These tables look great. But in most cases, the frames are weak, the leg attachments are thin metal or softwood, the tables are difficult (if not impossible) to level, and after a year of so of use, the laminated wood panels and legs crack, split, and peel.

The hardware—nuts, bolts, screws, etc.—are usually inferior, non-hardened metal, so they break and strip easily. The rail lug nuts (whether inserted or exterior) are thin, and can be cross-threaded and stripped effortlessly.

Just remember, you get what you pay for.

Positive: Asian imports are inexpensive, they have a good-looking finish, and the aprons are permanently attached to the rail.

Negative: Three rail bolt system. Inferior three-ply plywood is used for slate backing material, as are metal leg mounts.

Web site: ebay.com

AMERICAN HEIRLOOM: Rank 7-8

Beautifully designed and crafted tables, and are some of the most unique tables available.

Positive: The cabinets and rails are all hardwood constructed (no pressed woods, veneers, etc.) with 2" corner blocks and gussets for leg mounts, and exotic woods with excellent finishes.

Negative: Some of the wooden braces are only glued and stapled (instead of screwed), so don't always hold.

Web site: ahpooltables.com

AMERICAN HERITAGE: Rank 5-7

Very good cabinets on their top end tables, and okay to good cabinets on their low end tables. All wood leg attachment with gusset plates.

Positive: Inexpensive, they have a good-looking finish, and the aprons are permanently attached to the rail. Some models have wood leg mounting plates.

Negative: Three rail bolt system. Fiberboard (they call it Magna-Board) slate foundation, and in some cases no slate backing material. Some have metal leg mounting plates.

Web site: americanheritagebilliards.com

AMF: Rank 8-9

AMF has been in and out of the pool table business since the late 1950's. They make top-quality tables, with solid wood cabinets, and good slate and cushions.

The models in their Renaissance line are excellent, and the midrange Highland models are very good. (However, I'd stay away from the Playmaster models, better values can be found, see Playmaster below.)

Older AMF tables made in the nineteen fifties and sixties were built in the tradition of grand quality of that era, and are usually worth a look when thinking of a used table.

Positive: All wood construction.

Negative: Three rail bolt system, even on their nine-foot tables.

Web site: amfbilliards.com

BEACH: Rank 7-8

Beach Manufacturing has been making pool tables for over 50 years. They still use selected hard woods with rich finishes, and premium quality slate and cushions.

The quality of Beach tables has soared in recent years. New all-wood Beach tables are worth a look.

Positive: All wood construction.

Negative: Three rail bolt system, even on their nine-foot tables.

Web site: beachbilliards.com

BERINGER: Rank 7-9

Beringer tables are made in Canada. Most models are constructed from fine woods like mahogany with six-inch wide rails, and solidly mounted legs.

Positive: All wood construction.

Negative: Three rail bolt system, even on their nine-foot tables.

Web site: beringerbilliard.com

BOSTON TABLES: Rank 5

Imported from Asia. Watch for split legs and cabinet panels, and metal leg mounts.

Positive: Asian imports are inexpensive, they have a good-looking finish, and the aprons are permanently attached to the rail.

Negative: Three rail bolt system. Inferior three-ply plywood is used for slate backing material, as are metal leg mounts.

Web site: bostontables.com

BRUNSWICK: Rank 3-9

Started by Moses (love the name) Brunswick in 1845, Brunswick is the oldest billiard company in the U.S. and they make some fine high-quality tables. Of course, from a playability standpoint, because they certainly aren't pretty, the Gold Crown set the 9 ranking standard in 1958—even surpassing most antique tables—and hasn't been matched since, although the Gold Crown IV is its descendent and hangs close.

Most of today's Brunswick tables are excellent, made with quality woods with fantastic finishes, and fall in the 7-8 categories. However, I don't like a couple of their imports, especially those with metal leg attachment brackets, and would give those a 5 ranking, along with other Asian imports.

Brunswick also made the Bristol and a honeycomb model of a few years ago, and those should be ranked with a 1—they were so bad there may be only a few left. Brunswick still makes the Bristol, the Geneva, and a couple similar tables. In the last few years, they have improved these tables immensely by replacing particle board components with wood, so the ranking is boosted to the 4-5 category.

Positive: All wood construction, and great finishes of their top end tables. Excellent cushion when they use their Superspeed rubber.

Negative: Three rail bolt system, even on their nine-foot tables. Particle board (or no backing) is used on some slates.

Web site: brunswickbilliards.com

BRUNSWICK-BALKE-COLLENDER: Rank 7-8

Brunswick-Balke-Collender are antique Brunswick tables. Any all-wood antique table will rank high, but some of these old tables were veneered, with T-rails that don't necessarily give the best rebounds. Also, look for split and warped wood, and shale(ing) or flaking slate.

Brunswick has pictures and a short history of their antique tables on their web site.

Positive: They are antiques, some of them are gorgeous, and their value continues to climb.

Negative: Side mounted T-rails.

Web site: brunswickbilliards.com

C. L. BAILEY: Rank 6-7

Started in 1999, Bailey is becoming a very good table manufacturer. Their tables range from laminated plywood to solid hardwood construction. They also carry a line of imports, and are the distributor for Fischer pool tables.

Positive: Top end table are all wood construction.

Negative: Three rail bolt system.

Web site: clbailey.com

CONNELLY: Rank 6-9

Since 1980, each Connelly table has been built to standards that meet or exceed BCA specifications. Connelly tables come in six different sizes and thirty models, from entry level to professional, with thirteen good finishes.

Their all-wood Ultima is one of the best-made tables available, and even their low end; laminated tables have wood leg plates for a solid, no wobble, attachment.

In recent years, Connelly has added an exceptional cushion and four rail bolts to all their table rails for superior rebounds.

Positive: Four rail bolt system on all their new tables. All wood construction on their top end models. All wood leg mountings.

Negative: Particle board slate backing.

Web site: connellybilliards.com

DIAMOND: Rank 8-9

Founded in 1987 with its expressed goal of making the perfect pool table, Diamond has fast become one of the leaders in pool table design and manufacturing. They make a line of tables from home models to professional models, and all are all wood tables—no plywood or laminated surfaces are used on any Diamond table.

Positive: All wood construction.

Negative: Three rail bolt system, even on their nine-foot tables.

Web site: diamondbilliard.com

DYNAMO / VALLEY: Rank 6

It's hard to rank a coin-operated table above 5 because of the one-piece slate design; and Dynamo and Valley are almost identical. If the cabinet is one of the all wood boxes it makes an okay table, but a lot of earlier tables were constructed with particle board rails and cabinets.

Positive: For a coin-operated table, they are hard to beat if the cabinets are all wood.

Negative: Undersize slate; the rails are attached to the frame, not the slate.

Web site: vdlp.org

EMPIRE (POOL WORLD): Rank 4

Most Empire tables are built of plywood and (or) particle board and laminated with Formica or some other plastic, and most have a one-piece slate playing surface.

Positive: Slate table.

Negative: One-Piece, undersize slate with laminated plywood cabinets, and rails that attach to the frame.

Web site: poolworld.net

FISCHER: Rank 4

The original Fischer has been out of business for several years, although there are still a few of their tables floating around. Most Fischer tables were built from plywood and veneered with Formica.

Today, Fischer tables are imported from Asia and are distributed by C. L. Bailey Company.

Positive: Inexpensive.

Negative: The older tables were one-piece, undersize slate, with the rails attached to the frame. Newer tables are Asian imports with their anomalies.

Web site: clbailey.com

GANDY: Rank 7-8

After a hundred years in the business, Gandy closed their doors a few years ago. Most of their tables were made of poplar and veneered with Formica. Most Gandy models were good to very good tables.

Positive: Heavy, stiff frames made of poplar on their top models.

Negative: Three rail bolt system, even on their nine-foot tables. Laminates and veneers were used on most tables. Rail lug nuts stripped easily.

GOLDEN WEST: Rank 7-8

Golden West has been around since the late 1960's. They still do their own designing, manufacturing, laminating, and woodworking in-house. From Classic to Contemporary, they make very good tables with $1^{1}/_{4}$" cabinet panels and $1^{3}/_{8}$" wood leg plates for a solid leg attachment.

Positive: All wood construction on their top models with heavy wood leg attachments.

Negative: Laminates and particle boards used on some models, and for slate backing material. Three rail bolt system.

Web site: billiardmfg.com

HARVARD: Rank 1

Harvard tables are cheap, department store tables. They are made of particle board and fiber board, even the playing surface in most cases, which they call Slatron. Slatron is a fiberboard compressed with resin to help prevent warpage, and is guaranteed to remain level within the thickness of a dime. That's pretty poor.

Harvard tables are sold through Sears and other department stores under the Mezerak name.

Positive: Inexpensive.

Negative: All particle board tables.

Web site: escaladesports.com

IMPERIAL: Rank 5

Imported from Asia. Watch for split legs and cabinet panels, and metal leg mounts.

Positive: Asian imports are inexpensive, they have a good-looking finish, and the aprons are permanently attached to the rail.

Negative: Three rail bolt system. Inferior three-ply plywood is used for slate backing material, as are metal leg mounts.

Web site: imperialusa.com

KASSON: Rank 6-7

Kasson began in the early 1980s. Their top-end tables have interlocking, laminated hardwood subframes with solid maple leg gussets. But they still use a 3-bolt rail system.

Their low-end "home" tables are laminated plywood.

Positive: Solid wood constructed.

Negative: Three rail bolt system.

Web site: Kassonpooltables.com

MURRAY: Rank 1-5

Most Murray tables are playable. I have ranked most coin-operated tables 5 because of the one-piece slate design.

Murray's outdoor table is inferior to poor; because it's constructed mostly of plywood and fiberboard.

Positive: Inexpensive.

Negative: Three-rail bolt system. Often using lag or wood screws.

Web site: escaladesports.com

NATIONAL: Rank 1-5

National used to be an outstanding table. An original National table, reconditioned, would make an excellent choice.

Today, National pool tables are Murrey brand tables; with these tables think Asian imports.

Positive: Inexpensive.

Negative: Three-rail bolt system. Often uses lag or wood screws.

Web site: nationalpooltables.com

080 STUDIO: Rank 7

080 Studio makes a high-tech looking metal frame pool table with hardwood or metal rails. The table is excellently made but way overpriced for the average consumer.

Positive: All metal and solid.

Negative: Three-rail bolt system.

Web site: 080.com

OLHAUSEN: Rank 6-7

Started in 1973, Olhausen has grown rapidly.

A lot of Olhausen tables are built with particle board cabinets, blinds, and legs, with $^3/_4$" leg plate attachments simply stapled onto the bottom of the cabinet. Their top rails and cushions are their saving grace.

Positive: Their Acc-fast cushions are excellent.

Negative: Three rail bolt system, even on their nine-foot tables. Particle board slate backing.

Web site: olhausenbilliars.com

PLAYCRAFT: Rank 3-5

Imported from Asia. Watch for split legs and cabinet panels, and metal leg mounts.

Positive: Asian imports are inexpensive, they have a good-looking finish, and the aprons are permanently attached to the rail.

Negative: Three rail bolt system. Inferior three-ply plywood is used for slate backing material, as are metal leg mounts.

Web site: playcraft.com

PLAYMASTER: Rank 4-5

Playmaster is brought to you by AMF, but they're not in the same class.

Positive: Inexpensive.

Negative: Three rail bolt system, and lots of fiberboard (MDF—Medium Density Fiberboard).

Web site: amfbilliards.com

PROLINE: Rank 6-7

Started in 1976, ProLine began as very good tables and so far hasn't faltered. They have a large selection of wood tables with a large selection of furniture finishes. From contemporary to custom (although not really custom), they are very good tables.

Positive: All wood construction.

Negative: Three rail bolt system, even on their nine-foot tables. Particle board slate backing.

Web site: prolinebilliards.com

SEARS: Rank 1-2

For Sears or Mizerak tables see Harvard above.

Positive: Inexpensive.

Negative: All particle board tables.

Web site: sears.com

SCHMIDT: Rank 7-8

Schmidt began making tables in the late 1800s and made some very good tables—poplar frames, all wood rails, excellent finishes, and so forth. They still do.

Positive: Their top end models were constructed of all wood. All aprons on their newest tables were permanently attached to the rails. All wooden table parts are made in the U. S., and they use no particle board.

Negative: Three rail bolt system, even on their nine-foot tables.

Web site: schmidtpool.com

SHOWOOD: Rank 6-7

Showood started making tables for Olhausen in 1991, then went off on their own. They make good tables, but their veneer and traditional cabinet tables are hard to tell from Olhausen, or most other manufacturers in the same class.

Positive: Top models are well constructed and all wood. Their tables are still made in the U. S.

Negative: Three rail bolt system, even on their nine-foot tables. Particle board slate backing.

Web site: showood.com

STEEPLETON: Rank 6-8

Started in 1910, Steepleton is becoming one of the older manufacturers. They have always insisted on using high quality materials on their tables, although some are laminated plywood.

Positive: Top models are well constructed and all wood.

Negative: Three rail bolt system, even on their nine-foot tables. Particle board slate backing.

Web site: steepleton.com

VITALIE: Rank 7-8

For years, although overrated and overpriced, Peter Vitalie made very good tables, but their mid-range tables were priced in the high-range level. Watch for slate cracks on their older models.

Today's, Vitalie tables, however, are high-range tables, priced in the stratosphere.

Positive: Top models are well-constructed and all wood, with excellent finishes. All wooden parts are made in the U. S.

Negative: Three rail bolt system, even on their nine-foot tables. Fiberboard (MDF) slate backing.

Web site: vitalie-manufacturing.com

WHOLESALE BILLIARDS USA: Rank 5-6

Very good cabinets on their top end tables, and okay to good cabinets on their low end tables. All wood leg attachment with gusset plates.

Positive: Inexpensive, they have a good-looking finish, and the aprons are permanently attached to the rail. Some models have wood leg mounting plates.

Negative: Three rail bolt system. Fiberboard (they call it Magna-Board) slate foundation, and in some cases no slate backing material. Most models are imported components form Asian

Web site: wholesalebilliards.com

WORLD OF LEISURE: Rank 6-8

World of Leisure makes a line of tables that are good, but their veneer and traditional cabinet tables are hard to tell from most other manufacturers in the same class.

Positive: Top models are well constructed and all wood.

Negative: Three rail bolt system, even on their nine-foot tables. Particle board slate backing.

Web site: worldofleisuremfg.com

Z-BILLIARDS: Rank 3-5

Imported from Asia. Watch for split legs and cabinet panels, and metal leg mounts.

Web site: z-billiards.com

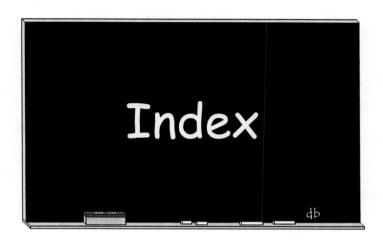

Index

ABOUT THE AUTHOR

After three years in the U.S. Army's 101st Airborne division (1962-1965) jumping out of perfectly good airplanes and working on Huey helicopters, I married, had two daughters then attended Indiana University's School of Business in Bloomington, Indiana.

After Indiana University, I opened a twenty-four table pool room in Indiana where I played on, sold, and serviced a variety of new, used, and antique tables.

In 1982, with one daughter in college and the other in high school, we moved to Arizona where I have remained in the pool table service and repair business.

My wife of thirty plus years and I now have two granddaughters and two grandsons.

Wow.

GIVE A GIFT THAT WILL BE APPRECIATED FOR YEARS

A Rookie's Guide to
Pool Table Maintenance and Repair
A Manual for Assembling, Re-covering,
Re-cushioning, Leveling, and Repairing

A Rookie's Guide to
Playing Winning Pool
From Beginning to Advanced Players

A Rookie's Guide to
Pool Table Assembly
Detailed and Illustrated Instructions
for Most Pool Tables

CHECK WITH YOUR FAVORITE BOOKSTORE, ONLINE BOOKSELLER BILLIARD SUPPLIER, OR

ON LINE
www.phoenix**billiards**.com
or
www.rookies-guide.com

GIVE A GIFT THAT WILL BE APPRECIATED FOR YEARS

A Rookie's Guide to
Pool Table Maintenance and Repair
A Manual for Assembling, Re-covering,
Re-cushioning, Leveling, and Repairing

A Rookie's Guide to
Playing Winning Pool
From Beginning to Advanced Players

A Rookie's Guide to
Pool Table Assembly
Detailed and Illustrated Instructions
for Most Pool Tables

CHECK WITH YOUR FAVORITE
BOOKSTORE, ONLINE BOOKSELLER
BILLIARD SUPPLIER, OR

ON LINE
www.phoenix**billiards**.com
or
www.rookies-guide.com